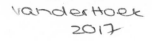

CAMPAIGN BOOT CAMP 2.0

☆ ☆ ☆ ☆ ☆ ☆ ☆

CAMPAIGN
BOOT CAMP 2.0

Basic Training for Candidates, Staffers,
Volunteers, and Nonprofits

CHRISTINE PELOSI

BK°

Berrett–Koehler Publishers, Inc.
San Francisco
a BK Currents book

Berrett-Koehler Publishers, Inc.
235 Montgomery Street, Suite 650
San Francisco, CA 94104-2916
Tel: (415) 288-0260   Fax: (415) 362-2512   www.bkconnection.com

Ordering Information
Quantity sales. Special discounts are available on quantity purchases by corporations, associations, and others. For details, contact the "Special Sales Department" at the Berrett-Koehler address above.
Individual sales. Berrett-Koehler publications are available through most bookstores. They can also be ordered directly from Berrett-Koehler: Tel: (800) 929-2929; Fax: (802) 864-7626; www.bkconnection.com.
Orders for college textbook/course adoption use. Please contact Berrett-Koehler: Tel: (800) 929-2929; Fax: (802) 864-7626.
Orders by U.S. trade bookstores and wholesalers. Please contact Ingram Publisher Services: Tel: (800) 509-4887; Fax: (800) 838-1149; E-mail: customer.service@ingrampublisherservices.com; or visit www.ingrampublisherservices.com/Ordering for details about electronic ordering.

Berrett-Koehler and the BK logo are registered trademarks of Berrett-Koehler Publishers, Inc.

Printed in the United States of America

Berrett-Koehler books are printed on long-lasting acid-free paper. When it is available, we choose paper that has been manufactured by environmentally responsible processes. These may include using trees grown in sustainable forests, incorporating recycled paper, minimizing chlorine in bleaching, or recycling the energy produced at the paper mill.

Library of Congress Cataloging-in-Publication Data
Pelosi, Christine.
    Campaign boot camp 2.0 : basic training for candidates, staffers, volunteers, and nonprofits / Christine Pelosi. -- 2nd ed.
       p. cm.
    ISBN 978-1-60994-516-9 (pbk.)
    1. Political campaigns--United States. 2. Political leadership--United States. 3. Politics, Practical--United States. I. Title.
    JK2281.P39   2012
    324.70973--dc23   2011051441

First Edition
17   16   15   14   13   12   10   9   8   7   6   5   4   3   2   1

Production: BookMatters; copyedit: Tanya Grove; proofing: Janet Reed Blake; index: Leonard Rosenbaum; text design: Bea Hartman; cover design: Irene Morris

To Isabella

Contents

Introduction   1

PART I ★ MESSAGE

1 Identify Your Call to Service   11
2 Define Your Message   48

PART II ★ MANAGEMENT

3 Know Your Community   79
4 Build Your Leadership Teams   101

PART III ★ MONEY

5 Raise the Money   135

PART IV ★ MOBILIZATION

6 Connect with People   161
7 Mobilize to Win   189

After-Action Review   219
Notes   223
Acknowledgments   229
Index   231
About the Author   241

Introduction

My political activism began in the stroller. Every year, right before Halloween, my mom took us door to door through our neighborhood with election leaflets. Then a few days later we returned for trick-or-treating. To this day, we are not entirely sure whether those leaflets had any bearing on the kind of treats we received. Maybe all that excess chocolate from certain neighbors was a coincidence.

It was unfathomable to us then that she would become Speaker of the House of Representatives nearly forty years later. But politics isn't about the big leap to power; it's about the thousands of steps taken with family, friends, and neighbors every day, from voting to volunteering to full-time civil, military, and political service. Millions of Americans have heeded a personal call to service: a voice of conscience that springs from vision, ideas, and values and urges participation. For many of us, activism begins with the rhythms of family traditions in civic, political, or faith-based action before we hear a singular beat that resonates. Now a mother myself, I am taking my daughter in her stroller to neighborhoods around the country engaging in participatory democracy. My lesson to her and to others: answer your call to service, follow your passion, and send your message to the future *today*.

Campaign Boot Camp 2.0 has emerged from my own call to service as a lifelong grassroots activist in politics and policy. From the stroller, I have enjoyed the engagement of campaigns, the excitement of current events, and the empowerment of using my voice and my vote to make a difference. Walking precincts, practicing law for the City of San Francisco, studying legislation while serving in the Clinton-Gore administration and on Capitol Hill, winning campaigns for Democratic Party office, and managing political organizations have given me the opportunity to work with thousands of people committed to fulfilling their dreams and imprinting their humanity on our society. I've been on the road in blue, red, and purple states for historic Democratic victories in 2006 and 2008, heartbreaking defeats in 2010, and resurgence in 2011. All the way through, the common thread has been a fight for progressive values and participatory democracy: elections come and go, official power comes and goes, issues fade. My call to service endures.

Why a "campaign"? Meeting the challenges that America faces depends on our participation in our democracy. Performing service, and attracting others to it, requires a *campaign*—a mechanism to work with people in a disciplined way toward a common goal. A campaign can be an effort to be elected to office, to build capacity for a nonprofit, or to increase legislative recognition of civil rights. Whatever form it takes, a winning political campaign is a fusion of a large social movement and a small-business start-up. It takes a long-term dedication to values and a short-term, nuts-and-bolts strategy to earn the votes needed to win come Election Day.

Why a "boot camp"? Public service requires identifying and harnessing the inspiration, perspiration, and perseverance that transform dreams into actions. In my experience elections are like graduations—some folks come magna cum laude and others come "lawdy, lawdy." The more magna cum laude campaigns out there with candidates and volunteers trained to put their best feet forward, the more vibrant and effective their service will be.

This is where the *boot camp* format—short, concentrated training sessions that respect people's time by providing questions and tools that hone skills and talent—comes in. We focus on a core curriculum of *message, management, money,* and *mobilization* to help people learn from others' successes and failures. I used this format with the AFSCME PEOPLE/New House PAC Congressional Candidates Boot Camp. The American Federation of State County Municipal Employees (AFSCME) Public Employees Organized to Promote Legislative Equality (PEOPLE) convened boot camps with over 100 challengers and twenty-six members of congress from 2006 to 2011. My leadership boot camps have included seminars, regional round tables, a University of California at Berkeley Extension class called Public Service Leadership Boot Camp, and several Young Democrats of America trainings on creating jobs, performing community service and outreach, building labor coalitions, and keeping America safe and free.

My material for boot camps comes in part from the opportunities I've had to travel around the country following my two passions: baseball and politics. In 1993 I toured baseball parks while awaiting the results of the California bar exam, traveling to over twenty ballyards and following my beloved San Francisco Giants to four of them along the way. From 2005 to 2011, I visited over thirty states conducting campaign boot camps. Both tours allowed me a community-based introduction to the American people. On my 1993 baseball tour, I studied the architecture of the ballparks, the lore of the game, and the pride of the communities, paying special attention to the game's fundamentals—teamwork, hitting, pitching, and fielding—without which no team can win.

On my political tours (which happily included a little baseball on the side), the stakes were considerably higher, but my approach was similar. I studied the architecture of the campaigns, the lore of political traditions, and the pride of the communities, paying special attention to campaign fundamentals—message, management, money, and mobilization—without which no campaign can win.

Sitting at a candidate rally is similar to sitting in a ballyard. Both give you the opportunity to assess the technical metrics and reflect on the intangibles—what politics calls "character" and baseball calls "make-up"—you look for in your heroes and admire even in your opponents.

As a baseball fan, I know that some of the best advice about hitting comes from the other team's pitcher. That's why as a proud Democrat I'm telling my story and learning from conservative Republicans and not just other progressives. Good organizing ideas come from institutions and from start-ups; from adopting childhood traditions and from rebelling against them; from friends and from opponents. As a prosecutor in San Francisco, I often sought advice on how to evaluate and try cases from defense attorneys. As chief of staff on Capitol Hill for Congressman John F. Tierney, Democrat of Massachusetts, I learned management techniques from a campaign management manual issued by the office of Congressman Dick Armey, Republican of Texas. I blog regularly at the *Huffington Post* and POLITICO's *Arena*, two venues where a variety of political views stimulate conversation and cross-training.

After campaigning across America in 2005 and 2006, I wrote the first edition *Campaign Boot Camp: Basic Training for Future Leaders* to capture the best practices on strategy and tactics from Democrats, Republicans, and Independents. *Campaign Boot Camp 2.0* builds on the first edition by including insights from the dozens of boot camps and trainings I have conducted with first-time candidates, staff, volunteers, nonprofits, and students from 2007 to 2011. It includes more information about leadership attributes, ethics, and strategies in the brave new world of online politics, social networks, and electronic interdependence.

What has changed over the last five years? In 2006, while there was a broad range of issues that moved voters, *nothing* shaped the perceptions of the people I met on the campaign trail more than the events of Hurricane Katrina and the Iraq War. In 2008, a bit of Bush fatigue and a protracted Democratic primary ushered in Democratic President Barack Obama. In 2010, Tea Party Republicans swept much of the country fueled by an enthusiasm gap over Democrats due to a 9 percent unemployment rate through which progressive messages were unable to penetrate. In 2011, Tea Party overreach in restricting workers' rights, women's health, and voters' protections awakened progressives who organized to fight anti-labor laws in Wisconsin and Ohio, defend Planned Parenthood, and literally Occupy Wall Street.

Looking to 2012, redistricting (which alters all state legislative and congressional district lines) and recession (which still affects too many families) will contribute to a fourth straight change election. Americans are anxious about the fragile markets for jobs, housing, and stocks. Middle-class families have already exhausted their coping mechanisms: women have entered the workforce, just about everyone is working longer hours at higher productivity for stagnant or lower pay, and homes are mortgaged to the hilt. Slow growth plus rising unemployment have eroded consumer confidence and increased exasperation at any politicians who do not appear to be working as hard to create jobs as people are working to find them.

We know that the two major parties will be rocked by this change election. The Tea Party will play a significant role in nominating the 2012 Republican candidate for president and continue to affect legislative races. The Occupy movement has captured the frustrations of working people fed up with waiting for Wall Street bailouts to trickle down to Main Street, yet whether that translates into coalitions that occupy the voting booth for Democrats (or anyone else for that matter) remains to be seen.

What we do know is that, quite simply, millions of people believe the American Dream is out of reach and under attack—and have decided to make incumbents and institutions pay the price. We are experiencing a cultural phenomenon and a political

power shift: beyond left and right, the fight is bottom-up versus top-down, ranging from progressives quoting the old Hopi
Indian prayer: "We are the ones we have waited for" to Tea
Partiers saying, "There is no one Tea Party leader—we are all
leaders." An illustration for the visually inclined: in the twen-
tieth century, the blackberry was a fruit and the beehive was a
hairdo. Now, in the twenty-first century, the blackberry is one
of many handheld technology tools that connect people, and the
beehive is a social networking model—a series of concentric circles linking technology, coalitions, and human networks—that
has replaced the old hierarchical pyramid. The beehive model
maximizes personal participation, creativity, and impact. It also
poses leadership challenges for longtime politicians or business
leaders who came up the old way, because there are no more
filters or layers that buffer them from public opinion. Today's
leaders have to adapt to this new reality: prepare to lose control
and listen to the wisdom of crowds.

Adapting to this political and economic turmoil—in which no
incumbency is safe, no nonprofit is sure of its funding stream,
and no true leader is buffered from the public—means that
aspiring public leaders will have to work harder and smarter in
leaner and meaner times to gain trust and contribute to a culture of service where we ask the best of people. Working harder
and smarter means having the grace and guts to make strategic
choices about message, management, money, and mobilization,
and to implement them under pressure. The strategic choices
include whether to attract innovators and take risks against the
establishment to define your message, whether to make pledges
to special interest groups when you seek endorsements and
money; whether to use one-to-many television ads or many-to-
many social media messaging; and, how to mobilize supporters
based upon those choices.

In my many interviews, a common theme from Democrats,
Republicans, and Independents was this: two kinds of people
enter public life—those who want to *do* something and those

who want to *be* something. *Campaign Boot Camp 2.0* is for people who want to *do* something. It's basic training for future leaders who hear a call to service and are looking for a roadmap of how to transform dreams into actions through connecting with people and organizing with social networks, nonprofits, and policy initiatives. It sets forth seven essential steps: Identify Your Call to Service, Define Your Message, Know Your Community, Build Your Leadership Teams, Raise the Money, Connect with People, and Mobilize to Win. Each chapter concludes with a Get Real exercise to personalize and integrate these ideas into your own scope of service. *Campaign Boot Camp 2.0*'s online home, www.PelosiBootCamp.com, provides additional training resources and blog postings. Throughout the book you'll find testimonials from prominent leaders about their calls to service.

Whether you're a young mom leafleting your neighborhood, an aspiring public leader, or a veteran politician, *Campaign Boot Camp 2.0* will help you answer your call to service, follow your passion, and send your message to the future *today*.

PART I

MESSAGE

ONE

Identify Your Call to Service: Your Message to the Future

The future belongs to those who believe
in the beauty of their dreams.

ELEANOR ROOSEVELT

The beauty of our founders' dreams is set forth in the Preamble to the U.S. Constitution:

> We the people of the United States, in order to form a more perfect union, establish justice, insure domestic tranquility, provide for the common defense, promote the general welfare, and secure the blessings of liberty to ourselves and our posterity do ordain and establish this Constitution for the United States of America.

Our democracy is a call to reimagine the founders' vision for America through the years. It requires a binding commitment between people, a commitment that begins with the earliest actions in family, school, worship, and community. It is a commitment that develops over time and experience, based on a call to service—the vision, ideas, and values that motivate each public servant.

Each of us has a personal call to service that motivates and inspires our actions in family, community, and public life.

Whether your public service involves helping a nonprofit agency achieve its mission, voting or volunteering in an election, mastering the skills of running for public office, studying political science and civics, or networking with your peers in a community improvement project, everything you do to engage in democracy begins with your call to service. Your call to service springs from your vision for the future, the values that drive it, the ideas that embody it, and your commitment to work in a community with others to achieve it. Your call to service is your message to the future.

Whether your household is grounded in social responsibility, politics, workers' rights, civil rights, or military service, your call begins at home with a family ethic, manifests itself in community work, and provides a touchstone for all you do, inspiring you on the good days and strengthening you on the bad days.

Many Americans find our personal calls to service inspired by the national vision, values, and ideas framed by our founders and realized by succeeding generations. We share a common American Dream yet have the freedom to express our personal interpretations of that vision. To many, that goes without saying, but when we consider the bloodshed of recent democratic reform movements in countries like Egypt, Tunisia, Libya, and Syria, we Americans can never take our individual liberty for granted.

Why answer the call to service? For many people the answer is to help others: to give back to a country that has given them opportunity or to help people achieve their stake in the American Dream. Volunteerism is the backbone of society: nothing happens in politics or community life without it. A secondary reason is that we help others in order to help ourselves: we build confidence and self-esteem through accomplishment; we connect with others, including role models or mentors; and we gain valuable experience for a job or business opportunity. Nothing is more satisfying than identifying your call to service, following your passion, and making a difference in the lives of others.

As President Barack Obama often says, success is measured by "progress for the American people."[1]

In assessing your own participation in our democracy, the first essential question is what is your personal call to service?

ARTICULATE YOUR VISION FOR THE FUTURE

For many, the call to service springs from a vision of America as a better place. What change do you want? In reading the Preamble to our Constitution, what resonates? What compels you to give your time, energy, and resources, and to stake your reputation? Consider what you have done in your community—with nonprofits, educational or religious organizations, civic associations, and political or cause-related campaigns. Go back and read essays you wrote for high school, college, or job applications: How did you describe yourself? What was your favorite job or volunteer activity? What was your major in school? Your most treasured campaign? Your best writing? A closer look will tell you the message you have been sending to the future.

COMMUNICATE THE IDEAS THAT
WILL REALIZE YOUR VISION

"Ideas have consequences," says columnist George F. Will, "large and lasting consequences."[2] Our Constitution was a bold stroke of ideas, imagination, and intellect that brought to life our founders' vision of the future. It continues to have global consequences.

My own call to service includes promoting democracy. During the tenth anniversary of the 9/11 terrorist attacks, the vision that kept coming to mind was a secure America where an engaged citizenry protects and defends our people and our Constitution. As the kids who were third graders on 9/11 are now young adults eligible to vote, I'd like to see them all registered and voting, and all serving their communities in national or civic service regardless of race, creed, nationality, gender, sexual orientation, or identity. I'd like to see the 9/11 generation of patriots come home to a society worthy of their sacrifice, with jobs, education, health care, and housing. I'd like a better balance of liberty and security for all Americans and an appreciation of our military as a force for good in the world.

Many ideas implicit in that vision require concrete answers. How do we share the sacrifice? Who is required or recruited or allowed to serve? How do we maintain force readiness and care for troops, military families, and veterans? How much of the federal budget do we spend in relation to all the other needs of the country? Do we raise taxes, and, if so, whose? Most important are the practical consequences: When and how do we propose to deploy the strong military to go to war and to protect us here at home? Should we continue with deployments to Iraq, Afghanistan, or other nations? Each answer has a large and lasting consequence.

ARTICULATE THE VALUES THAT
SHAPE YOUR VISION AND IDEAS

Just as integral to your vision of the future and your big ideas are the core values—such as equality, responsibility, and justice—that inspire the vision. Too often we jump into political discussions without articulating our values. We may assume that others know what we believe or impute a value to our action, but assuming is always a mistake.

If, to take my example, your vision is a secure America where an engaged citizenry protects and defends our people and our Constitution, and your idea is to provide for the common defense through a strong military, your values will shape your treatment of the military servicemen and servicewomen. Equality shapes who gets called to serve and how: Would you enforce a draft or keep military service voluntary? Are all people, regardless of race, gender, class, or sexual orientation welcome to serve? Responsibility shapes how you prepare them when you deploy them in harm's way at home or overseas. Justice guides whether you keep promises to military families and properly provide for veterans upon their return home.

TEST YOUR VISION, IDEAS, AND VALUES TO SEE THE DIFFERENCE THEY MAKE IN PEOPLE'S LIVES

So far we've been dealing with the imagination; your vision becomes real when you make choices in public life that make a difference in people's lives.

On a personal level, you might achieve your vision for a safer America, your idea of a strong military, and your values of equality, responsibility, and justice by enlisting in the military or by supporting the families of people who enlist. On a community level, you might achieve the vision by supporting initiatives to provide workforce training and small-business loans to veterans returning home.

How can you tell if a candidate shares your vision? Let's say, for example, that you were evaluating candidates for president, and several promise a vision of America with the idea of a strong military and the values of equality, responsibility, and justice. So far, so good, but who will achieve the vision in the manner you intend? Until a crisis brings it home, it's just a theory.

On a political level, you might volunteer to work for a candidate who shares your vision. However, two people with a shared vision can have vastly different values about how to get there. Consider the debate over the December 2010 repeal of the military's Don't Ask, Don't Tell (DADT) policy that prohibited gay and lesbian military servicemembers from serving openly in the U.S. armed forces.

To the vast majority of Americans, the votes to repeal DADT fit comfortably within the Pledge of Allegiance: "with liberty and justice for all." (Even conservative icon Barry Goldwater advocated for opening the military to gays as early as 1993: "You don't have to *be* straight to be in the military; you just have to be able to *shoot* straight.") While there must be work to achieve the vision of equality in deed as well as in law, at a time of war with a volunteer military comprised of only 3 percent of eligible servicemembers, most believed a DADT repeal could not come too soon. In addition, the Pentagon's 2010 Comprehensive

★ ★ ★ ★ ★ ★ ★ ★ ★ ★ ★

NORAD TEST: SEVEN MINUTES TO KNOW IF A PRESIDENTIAL CANDIDATE SHARES YOUR VISION

Before volunteering or voting for a presidential candidate, apply this NORAD test: Assume that, as happened on September 11, 2001, it takes about seven minutes from the time the North American Aerospace Defense Command (NORAD) gets word that the country is under attack to the time fighter jets arrive in response. If NORAD identifies a threat—a hijacked airplane or a missile over a densely populated area—should the president order the jets to fire? At whom? How many American lives are at risk on the plane or on the ground?

Picture yourself or a loved one on the plane, in the targeted area, or watching—safe from immediate harm—as the crisis unfolds. What do you want your president to do? What vision, ideas, and values do you want the president to apply in those seven minutes? Would it make any difference if the NORAD commander or the U.S. president were a woman? A member of a racial minority? Openly gay?

Although few other tests will be as dramatic, you must articulate your vision for the future, your ideas, and the values and code of ethics that guide your call to service and your decisions under fire to see how they will affect people's lives.

Source: National Commission on Terrorist Attack upon the United States, *The 9/11 Commission Report,* http://www.9-11commission.gov, p. 20.

Working Group report revealed that over two-thirds of service-members did not think ending this policy would have an impact on military cohesion and readiness.

However, there were others who disagreed because their values took them in another direction. A Pew poll taken in November 2010 found that liberal Democrats backed a repeal by 6 to 1. And two voter groups—the religiously unaffiliated and voters under 30—backed ending DADT in proportions almost as large.

By contrast, 52 percent of self-described conservative Republicans opposed a repeal and only 28 percent supported it, while among white evangelical Protestants, 48 percent opposed it and 34 percent supported it.[3] But note that many Republicans voted for the end of DADT and a handful of house Democrats voted against—proving that one's personal values and party affiliation are not one and the same.

BE PART OF SOMETHING
LARGER THAN YOURSELF

To experience the challenges and rewards of public service, and to find out what kind of engagement best suits your talents, work with people who share your vision, ideas, and values. Volunteer with a student organization, a community project, a nonprofit, or an election campaign. The way you act to achieve your vision is a signal to you and to others that you are engaged to *do* something: to make a difference in your community and make the future better.

In her best-selling book *Know Your Power*, my mother, U.S. House Democratic leader Nancy Pelosi, says if you hear a call or see a problem, "organize, don't agonize."[4] *Organize* means be part of something larger than yourself, work with others on their own paths to service, and remember that it is amazing how much you can accomplish if you are willing to share the credit.

You must do something for people before you ask them to do something for you. Think of it this way: if you had a friend who showed up only when she needed something or called only to ask you for money, you would probably not stay friends for long. The same is true in public life. Don't be a taker. If someone gives you the opportunity to serve, pay it forward by helping someone else get involved or by donating money or resources to improve an organization.

Volunteer. To get started, give your time as a volunteer. "Every job I got I volunteered first," recalled Lezlee Westine, a founder and former president of TechNet, a bipartisan network of technology companies designed to promote innovation and competitiveness. "You cannot underestimate the huge value of volunteering for your first job. Volunteering is a great opportunity to show your passion for a cause and catapults you faster to a leadership role in an organization."[5]

STRENGTHEN YOUR FRIENDSHIPS
AND ALLIANCES IN NETWORKS

As you articulate your vision, ideas, and values; as you begin the service that puts them into action; and as you emerge as a trustworthy policy advocate, you will develop friendships and alliances. Westine advises aspiring leaders to "build technology networks to bring people together, coalition networks to accomplish a policy goal, and human networks to advance and mentor other people."

Technology networks. Create technology networks through the Internet to organize local groups and individuals for fundraising, communicating with the public on a grassroots level without using traditional media, and targeting favorable voters for get-out-the-vote efforts.[6]

I saw many of these networks firsthand on the campaign trail these past few years. Many fresh recruits—from New Direction Democrats to Tea Party Republicans—were volunteers connected with partisan groups like Young Democrats and College Republicans. But just as significant were the people mobilized by progressive netroots (Internet-based grassroots organizers) such as MoveOn.org and the *Daily Kos* community, by conservative networks such as the Club for Growth, and by fiercely independent communities such as the Iraq and Afghanistan Veterans of America (IAVA).

This new blend of asymmetrical politics thrives on bringing old-school politics and new media together. In communities around the country, I visited with people who had lost confi-

★ ★ ★ CALL TO SERVICE ★ ★ ★

NANCY PELOSI

"Our diversity is our strength," says House Speaker Nancy Pelosi. Pelosi grew up in multiethnic Baltimore, where she heard the call to service as a young girl. Her family home was always open to constituents of her father, the late Mayor Thomas D'Alesandro Jr., and she attributes her call to service to her parents, who, she says "raised us to be proud of our Italian Catholic heritage, patriotic in our love of country, and respectful of other people's pride in their heritage."

"When people ask me why I serve, I always answer in the same way: our children, our children, our children: the air they breathe, the water they drink, the food they eat, their health and education, a world at peace in which to live, the job security of their parents and the retirement security of their grandparents. I see my own service as an extension of my role as a mother and a grandmother."

When asked how she handled being the subject of multimillion-dollar attack ads in 2010: "If I were not effective, if I hadn't passed health care and Wall Street [regulatory overhaul] and the rest, I would not have been the target that I was. I came here to do a job. I didn't come here to keep a job."

Source: Nancy Pelosi, interviews, July 14, 2007 and January 3, 2011.

dence in the large institutions yet felt intense pride in their own community institutions and service traditions. Not only were they voting out a culture of corruption, they were ushering in a culture of service: walking precincts for candidates and walking 10Ks for AIDS or breast cancer research; meeting to clean up politics and to clean up beaches, parks, and neighborhoods. American politics is being reinvigorated by these social networks of people willing to come together around a shared mission, stay together through challenges, and work together despite the inevitable clashes of personalities and agendas.

Coalition networks. Westine's service in the White House involved working with a series of coalition networks, which she describes as a "temporary alliance of groups to achieve a common goal." These coalition networks can include journalists, nongovernmental organizations, corporate executives, and political leaders—"groups of people with followings beyond themselves" organized around a specific policy objective.

Human networks. The most effective way to build a culture of service is to develop a network of people who share your call to service. For example, your call to service may be the economic empowerment of women. A women's business network will help achieve the vision because it will do the following: host fund-raisers for women candidates or candidates who champion issues important to women; lobby government by showcasing the impact of women-owned businesses in terms of numbers of workers and revenues; influence media coverage of the most powerful women business owners; support women for political positions; and encourage successful women to mentor younger women. "From handshaking to supporting your peers to supporting a candidate, human networks will advance your goals and have untold benefits," advises Westine.

Start building your human networks with the people whose leadership you admire. Work with a local nonprofit or political leader on a public service effort to learn the ropes, develop relationships, and take a shared risk.

Above all else, build connections and relationships—what Westine calls the glue that holds together any network.

To build networks, start with your call to service. Lead with your passion and ask yourself, "Which one of the issues or causes calls me to serve?" There are great online sources for finding volunteer opportunities and networks such as volunteermatch .com, school alumni associations, and local campaign offices.

Look into a particular group and ask: What is the reputation? Do people in it have fun? Do they make an impact? Are my friends involved? How would I fit in? Also consider the management style: the simple fact of having a Web site or Listserv doesn't tell you everything. Look deeper: consider whether the network is using the old top-down pyramid style or has adopted the modern beehive model. If there are still only a couple of decision makers who don't want volunteer feedback or who expect junior members to filter for them, you will not be as fulfilled as you will by the beehive model where every worker adds value, and leaders have learned to delegate, interact with supporters, and heed the wisdom of crowds.

You may be shy about putting yourself out there, but you may enjoy volunteering at a networking event, rather than attending as a guest. Can you work the phones or the doors? Can your business offer a service rather than cash? If you're not sure, take a risk! The worst that can happen is you help other people and decide that a particular task or group is not for you. Finding your own style will help maximize your impact and fulfillment.

Demonstrate that you want to DO something, not just BE something. Begin with a good work ethic so that you are known as a workhorse, not a show horse. We all know the difference between colleagues who contribute and those who sail in at the last minute to avoid the heavy lifting. Performing the basic tasks of campaigning—sorting mail, stuffing envelopes, answering phones, handing out leaflets, making calls, updating Web sites— gives you hands-on experience in mobilization and exposure to the areas of messaging, fund-raising, and media outreach. Your willingness to do the basic work tests your commitment to a cause and seeds the grassroots of future support.

Register to vote—and vote! Dozens of elected officials at all levels of government come up for reelection every two, four, or six years. In addition, ballot measures at the local and possibly state levels are subject to voter approval. These are all opportunities to learn. Register to vote and know where to vote. If you have moved, update your registration. Being registered to vote is not enough; studying the issues, comparing each candidate's position, and actually voting are critical for those considering a run for public office. Register other people to vote as well: encourage family and friends; register new citizens at their swearing-in ceremonies; and participate in voter registration drives.

Unhappy are the candidates who register or vote only shortly before running themselves and have to answer for the fact that they haven't voted when others were up for consideration. Republican candidates for California's biggest public offices in 2010—Meg Whitman for governor and Carly Fiorina for the senate—had spotty voting records that reinforced the notion that they weren't interested in politics unless they could start at the top. The public didn't trust them to grapple with tough issues as leaders since they hadn't grappled with those issues (abortion rights, immigration, taxes) as voters.

Train and be trained. You must excel in the core areas of public service: message, management, money, and mobilization. Challenge yourself. Many local nonprofit organizations and political parties sponsor training sessions for potential candidates and volunteers. Many of my leadership boot camps have included training materials and speakers from Democratic Party committees as well as AFSCME, AFL-CIO, Democracy for America, EMILY's List, Equality California, Fair Share Alliance, Human Rights Campaign, SEIU, Truman National Security Project, Veterans and Military Families for Progress, and the Women's Campaign Forum, each of whom perform their own trainings helping activists develop advocacy skills. Take courses that teach you how to write op-eds (from "opposite editorial" page), which you can submit to your local paper, and how to create presentations and informational videos that you can upload to YouTube.

Once you've recruited people, be sure to tweet them updates. Start an online group on LinkedIn, Facebook, Google Plus, or other social network, if none already exists that shares your vision, and invite people to join it. When I started boot camps in 2005, there were none I could find that performed cross-training among different groups, but just about everyone is conducting trainings these days. Be sure you get materials in advance and testimonials from those who have already participated to see what is worth your time and money, and check for interactivity and media training. Nothing solidifies your training better than having to stand up and talk about what you just learned.

If you are conducting trainings, be sure to invite people from different disciplines—business, labor, constituency groups—as well as at least one alum to come back as a presenter. We did this with our Congressional Candidates Boot Camps to show challengers that our message, management, money, and mobilization metrics are indeed keys to victory. After one boot camp, a candidate e-mailed me his feedback, concluding: "I am going to win and come back as a presenter." He did: our 2006 alum, Congressman Ed Perlmutter of Colorado, came back in subsequent years to affirm the importance of grassroots organizing. He told us that one reason he ran for Congress was to push for expanded research that could help cure his oldest daughter, who has epilepsy. After over a year of walking door to door to door talking about stem cell research and other issues of the day, Perlmutter built a commanding lead, attracted a large volunteer corps, won that election, and has won two others since. Perlmutter's simple and profound message: "I won because I walked."

Pay it forward: mentor people as people mentored you. Everybody got a start from somebody. Sharing information, imparting wit and wisdom, and offering unvarnished advice is essential. This can be as simple as a few words of encouragement or as committed as a decades-long advisory role. Anyone new to a job or a position needs to learn the ropes. When running for chair

of the California Democratic Party Women's Caucus in 2011, I
was nominated by my longtime mentor, Democratic National
Committeewoman Rosalind "Roz" Wyman, who has advised
me since I was her podium page when she ran the 1984 Democratic National Convention. Not only did I want people to hear
from a woman of great achievement in our state, I wanted my
caucus to know that we all still need advice and support from our
mentors. Our successful team of officers won on the WOMEN
Slate: Women Organizing Mentoring Electing and Networking.
Our pledge is to pay it forward; the women we mentor are our
messages to the future.

Match your skills to a position. Consider preparing yourself for
one of the campaign staff roles in an upcoming election. When
trying to make a match, identify your top five or ten experi-
ences from campaigning to carpooling to coaching. What do they
tell you about how you answered your call to service and how
you helped others? Do you like to be the disciplinarian or the
free spirit in the group? Leverage your participation: you don't
need to have political experience to be a good organizer with
a nonprofit or get an entry-level position with a political campaign. Are you a stay-at-home mom? You're an organizer. Have
you coached, worked on the PTA, or driven carpool? You're an
organizer. A careful look at your service contributions, lessons
learned, and value added will reveal your networks and (perhaps
hidden) talents.

Be part of a team. Networking requires you to work with and
for other people. Politics and policy are about teamwork. Some
people like to study, worship, and work alone; if you do, perhaps
a behind-the-scenes role is appropriate for you. Assuming you
enjoy the camaraderie and cooperation of a team effort, you will
be spending most of your time asking other people to volunteer
their time, write a check, bring their networks in common cause
with yours, and/or hire your candidate to work for them.

   If you decide to become a candidate or commissioner or nonprofit trustee, you will have a constituency to which you will have to answer, and each member of that constituency gets to vote on whether you get the job, has an opinion of how you are doing in the job, and ultimately decides whether you should keep the job. None of this will be communicated in the old hierarchical ways: any moment could bring a tweet or a message assessing your performance or offering new ideas. If you shy away from conflict or have slow response times, being out front is going to be a hard adjustment. On the other hand, if you are open to crowd sourcing, a network can help you assume a position of leadership based upon what you can contribute to the network.

Finally, campaigns are environments where the stakes are high and the pressure is intense. Networking means listening, and the feedback you hear will not always be favorable. You will have to hear criticism about work that springs from your intensely personal core vision, ideas, and values—and not take it personally. Remembering that you are a part of something larger than yourself will help you on the bad days—and even on the good days—to develop a thick skin.

WOMEN LEADERS:
CONSIDER YOURSELF ASKED

Women often find it harder to make the leap into campaigns because many of us remain the primary caregivers for our children and our parents, so family time is harder to let go. And public attitudes remain stereotypical, even among close supporters. I remember receiving an award at the pre-Columbus Day luncheon of the Irish-Israeli-Italian Society of San Francisco during my days as a deputy prosecutor. There I was, my speech all lined up about the caring traditions of Trócaire, Tikkun Olam, and Caritas when a family friend approached my table announcing loudly, "I'm praying for your husband." My response, thinking she mistook me for one of my married sisters: "It's Christine; I don't have a husband." "I know," she replied, "that's why I am

★ ★ ★ ★ ★ ★ ★ ★ ★ ★ ★

TIPS FOR WOMEN CANDIDATES: CONFRONTING STEREOTYPES

Gender bias is real. People will view your leadership through the lens of their perceptions.

You . . .	What They'll Say . . .
Single?	You can't attract 'em.
Married?	You should put 'em over career.
Got Kids?	You should stay home with 'em.
Divorced?	You couldn't keep 'em.
Widowed?	You killed 'em.

Don't let these perceptions silence you! Be ready to meet strangers and get out of your comfort zone. Prepare to be questioned about your life choices. Remember criticism and effectiveness go hand in hand. (Life's too short. . . .)

SHARE THE CREDIT: ". . . LIKE JANE SAID"

Other aspects of mentoring arise in the rough and tumble of competitive campaigns and high-level meetings. All too often I hear a version of this story: Jane articulates an idea. Joe repeats the idea. Others speak afterward and say, "Didn't Joe have a great idea?" or ". . . like Joe said." So it is up to someone to interject ". . . like Jane said" to give credit where it is due. A curious but common condition afflicts some people in which they seem to have an inability to hear something said by someone younger, by those lower on the professional ladder, or by people who are unlike them in some way.

praying for him!" My colleagues roared with laughter. One who has since gone on to elected office herself said, "When people ask me where my husband is, I say, 'I don't know, but if you find him tell him I'm looking for him.'"

It's not just pressure to have a family—it is pressure from

a family member. More recently, two female candidates dealt with family pressure. One was starting her campaign when her mother asked her, "Who'll take care of your children?" (Translation: "Not Grandma.") The other got a call from home that her daughter's response to mom contemplating a primary was to dye her hair "one of the primary colors." (Translation: "Mom, stay home.") These are quite legitimate issues—and ones we encounter every day. Primary caregivers of small children find that before we can accept any opportunity, our first question is about childcare. I traveled to over twenty states with my infant daughter, and each boot camp from halfway across my home-town to halfway around the world began with: "How will I care for Isabella?" One person asked me, "Why don't you bring your nanny?" "I am the nanny," I replied. Every primary care-giver has to answer that childcare question, so candidates must remember this is not a trick question, just a very public one.

A Brown University study addressed the issue of women candidates with a report that asked "Why Don't Women Run for Office?" The researchers found that women are less likely than men to have received the suggestion to run for office from party and elected officials, political activists, or family and friends; yet when women receive external support from formal and informal political and nonpolitical sources, they are twice as likely to run.[7]

Ellen Malcolm, founder of EMILY's List, a national network of 100,000 members who recruit, train, and support Democratic pro-choice women candidates, says the Brown study shows that people who care about public service should encourage others to run. The theory behind EMILY's List—EMILY stands for Early Money Is Like Yeast—is that early networking and institutional support helps the campaign "dough" rise. Malcolm says estab-lishing a pipeline for women to run is essential because "prog-ress doesn't happen in a moment, but in battle after battle for our values." Malcolm's message to potential candidates: "Con-sider yourself asked."[8]

This sentiment is echoed by Florida congressional candidate Annette Tadeo, now with the Women's Campaign Fund, who explained during our joint presentation to the Florida Young Democrats, "Women are not asked to run. A woman with a PhD in education won't run for School Board because she will think she is not qualified, but a man without that degree or kids in the school system will run. Because we need to encourage more women, the Women's Leadership Fund site established www .Sheshouldrun.com for people to nominate people (or themselves) to run."[9]

These networks are essential as women candidates and opinion leaders find the environment changing as the novelty of female leaders wears off. The feminist Barbara Lee Family Foundation commissioned a poll to study voter attitudes and research female candidates' campaigns. Some results are striking:

* Strong is likeable—voters decoupled strength and toughness.

* Voters like problem solvers and think women have more agility due to roles as moms and wives, though moms of small children were greeted more skeptically in terms of their time to do the job well.

* Voters assume honesty and punish perceived dishonesty.

* Likeability matters more for women candidates than men: negative campaigning may erode any gender advantage gained from being seen as more corroborative.[10]

FOLLOW YOUR PERSONAL CODE OF CONDUCT

First and foremost, you have to be yourself. All too often, people will get into trouble when, rather than being confident in their service mission, they adapt their views to more experienced people's in exchange for a possible advancement, endorsement, or contribution. Bad idea. Your stated values, ethics, and code of conduct should guide your behavior and your decisions on and off the campaign trail. First and foremost, you must be yourself and present the same call to service mission to everyone.

People may offer contributions to your organization, cause, or candidate, in exchange for a particular outcome. Stop the conversation. No contribution is worth your soul, much less your liberty and reputation. Other people may urge you to use negative information about the opposition or will tell unsavory details of their conversations with other people. A simple rule applies: "If they'll do it *for* you, they'll do it *to* you." Once you ditch your old supporters for new friends, your new friends will know how little you value friendship and could ditch you on the same grounds. Think long and hard before you abandon your values, your friends, or your commitments.

When you undertake the leadership of a campaign, you become responsible for anything that goes out to the public. Establish clear ethical standards and expectations for practices such as fact-finding and fund-raising, and clear policies for endorsements, questionnaires, and Internet use—*and stick to them.*

WALK YOUR TALK

"People want to see how you walk on this earth," explains international human rights activist Kerry Kennedy, president of the Robert F. Kennedy Center for Justice and Human Rights. How you walk your own talk will set the tone of your public service.

"Make an effort to do more than 'campaign' so that people can see who you are in your core," Kennedy advises. "Do something in your campaign that helps people and reflects your message." For example, her brother, former Congressman Joseph Kennedy, incorporated his message into a service: when going to senior centers to pitch health care, he would ditch the standard coffee and donuts for healthy snacks and an exercise routine of light calisthenics that he performed along with the crowd.[11]

If you are working on a political campaign or initiative to protect and preserve the environment, make your campaign carbon neutral, carpool, set up events near public transportation, recycle, and use recycled products. If you support workers rights in Wisconsin, Ohio, and across America, do not cross picket lines or patronize anti-union establishments. My husband and I have yet to celebrate our anniversary at the hotel where we married in 2008 because the management had a dispute with employees who in turn enlisted the Brass Liberation Orchestra for a flash mob dancing to a Lady Gaga-inspired song: "Don't Get Caught in a Bad Hotel." Now that there is labor peace we shall return, but for a while all we had was our wedding album and the flash mob's YouTube video.[12]

Organize public service events such as monthly volunteer clean-ups of a local park, beach, or community center. Be sure to pick up after yourself and others when you use public space. Every small gesture reinforces the larger message.

PERFORM AN ACT OF COURAGE
TO ACHIEVE YOUR VISION

The big test of your commitment to service will come when you have to risk your reputation and perform an act of courage to achieve your vision.

Meet people you don't know and ask them for help. Would you call people you don't know to ask them to hire someone? Would you call people you don't know and ask them to hire you? Would you go to the homes of people you don't know, knock on the door, and ask them to hire you or a friend? Think of your last job interview. Now imagine doing it every day walking door to door in your neighborhood. Think of your last performance evaluation. Now imagine it posted on the Internet, with an opportunity for anyone to post their comments. That is a flavor of the exposure you have as a public leader.

Get out of your comfort zone. Your base supporters are people who will walk precincts in the rain, talk to complete strangers, and sleep on floors for you—in other words, people who are willing to get out of their comfort zone for you or your cause. Think about it: for whom or what have you walked in the rain? Talked to strangers and received unvarnished feedback? Opened your home to a stranger or slept on a floor in another town? Getting out of your comfort zone is a true measure of commitment, and inspiring others to get out of their comfort zone is a true measure of leadership. Your comfort level in asking people to talk to strangers, walk in the rain, and sleep on the floors and/or your willingness to do these actions yourself will reveal what sort of role you want to take, either behind the scenes, out front for a cause, or as a candidate yourself.

Getting out of your comfort zone may mean that you buck your friends or your political party from the left or the right. Nowadays most candidates have Democrats for X Republican or Republicans for X Democrat committees to show cross-party appeal. Remember there were "Obamacons"—Conservatives for Obama—and Democrats for McCain in 2008. You might have a good friend who is running in a primary whom you want to support even though it will be an uphill or uncomfortable fight. Again, you take it back to your call to service: if this is what you consider the right thing to do, follow your passion and fight the good fight.

Take a political risk. You will face criticism and skepticism from people who think your ideas are unrealistic or politically impossible. In the immortal words of Eleanor Roosevelt, "Do what you feel in your heart to be right, for you'll be damned if you do and damned if you don't." I used that quote at a 2008 dinner to introduce then-San Francisco mayor (now California's Lt. Governor) Gavin Newsom, who took a political risk in 2004 when he decided to officiate over thousands of same-sex weddings much to the chagrin of those activists and politicians who wanted to wait for the courts to decide marriage equality.

More recently, California Attorney General Kamala D. Harris bucked the U.S. Department of Justice's 2011 push to settle

BURNS STRIDER:
BIG DADDY'S RULES OF THE ROAD

Before you get out and campaign, consider these words of wisdom from Burns Strider, a Democratic strategist with Capitol Hill experience in outreach to veterans, evangelical Christians, and rural areas. After advising House Democrats and Hillary Clinton's presidential campaign, Strider founded the Eleison Group, which practices what his Big Daddy used to preach about ethics and campaigning.

Most of the campaign rules I follow came from my father. He was known as Big Daddy by nearly everyone in Mississippi. He stood at 6'7"; weighed in at over 330 pounds; and wore a suit, cowboy hat, and cowboy boots seven days a week. He was sheriff of Grenada County for twenty-four years. With my brother currently in the sheriff's office we're still getting elected. I've spent my entire life going door to door asking for votes. By the time I was a teenager I knew everyone in Grenada. I knew who was kin, who had marriage plans. Heck, I knew those getting divorced—and usually why. I learned respect for folks. I learned about listening to people and taking them seriously.

BIG DADDY'S RULES OF THE ROAD

1. **A pickup truck beats a Cadillac every day of the week out here in real America.**

TRANSLATION: Don't get fancy. Don't get fancy with your words, with your plan, or with your attitude. Folks are looking for one of them to lead.

2. **Every tub has got to sit on its own bottom.**

TRANSLATION: In the final analysis, the candidate has to carry the day. The candidate is who the voters want to hear from. Only the candidate can speak for the candidate.

3. **If you're driving down the highway and see a car coming toward you in your lane, then you're going to change lanes.**

TRANSLATION: Don't get in the way of your friends. Stay out of other people's races. Stay in your lane and don't bring undue criticism and opposition by being nosy or getting involved where you shouldn't. ▶

▶ **4. If you come up on an old yella' mangy dog and that dog is barking the Gospel, then let him bark.**

TRANSLATION: Don't you challenge, denigrate, or dismiss the faith of anyone. A person's faith represents the core, the essence of who they are. It's one of their most personal choices. You tear that person down if you tear down their faith. Hell, join them. It can probably do you some good.

5. Be careful what you say about someone; you're probably talking to their cousin.

TRANSLATION: You're probably talking to their cousin.

6. In politics if you take a swing at someone, you better be prepared to take one right back.

TRANSLATION: If you're gonna' throw a punch, be ready to take a punch. I actually learned this one from Speaker Nancy Pelosi. Think down the road to where your decisions are taking you.

7. Decide what you're going to do, then say you're going to do it, go do it, and then come back and tell them you did it.

TRANSLATION: It's just not enough to believe it or even do it. This is another important rule from Speaker Pelosi. Politics and people must know where you stand on an issue. They must know your actions. Just doing something without getting the news out is a waste of good time.

8. Our veterans stood up for our nation with their lives. If you can't support veterans in your actions as well as your words then just stay on the damn front porch.

TRANSLATION: Pretty words are just that—pretty words. Saluting our veterans and troops must be based in real policy that will reap earned benefits for our veterans and military families—a new, stronger GI Bill of Rights, the end to the Disabled Veterans Tax, a fully funded VA health care system, and fully providing for the health care of our National Guard and Reservists.

Source: Burns Strider, "Big Daddy's Rules of the Road," *Trail Mix,* October 18, 2006; updated by e-mail, May 29, 2007.

with banks, holding out for more homeowners' recourse and consumers' protection. Bucking the tide meant that these young leaders chose to make some establishment figures quite uncomfortable, but they also gained legions of new admirers who saw their impatience as more fitting for the circumstances.

Newsom and Harris each made a personal decision to advance their visions, ideas, and values, and risked losing to advance a service mission.

Demonstrating the courage of your convictions sometimes means you make the fight, even if you are not likely to win or face steep odds. When it came to the health-care reform fight in 2009 and 2010, there were many Democrats who knew that this fight was as big as the fight for the New Deal and Social Security in the 1930s and the Voting Rights Act in the 1960s. As Arizona Congresswoman Gabby Giffords said in a March 2010 statement announcing her support for health-care reform: "The American people are being made to suffer through millions of dollars of corporate-sponsored distortions intended to scare the public and obstruct the progress of reforms."[13] She added: "As we approach this vote, I am acutely aware of the lobbying groups that do not support these reforms. What they cannot spin is who I am or the values that guide my decisions."

Americans saw what her Cactus Roots supporters knew about Giffords's values when she maintained her dignified demeanor after her office in Tucson was vandalized hours after the votes, saying, "Our democracy is a light, a beacon really, around the world, because we affect change at the ballot box and not because of these outbursts of violence in certain cases and the yelling."[14]

Challenge a sacred cow. Another way to take a political risk in the nonprofit context is to challenge a sacred cow. Do you serve on the board of a nonprofit where the overhead seems excessive compared to the services performed? The sacred cow may be perks for the directors or money spent according to the whims of powerful donors rather than according to a mission statement.

Or it may be paying large amounts of overhead for compara-tively little deliverables. In politics this could mean exposing gold-plated government contracts that are not put out for com-petitive bidding.

Taking on sacred cows is especially important for women leaders. Longtime political activist and 2012 Project director Mary Hughes, whose "dream work" is helping women achieve power, says bipartisan public polling reveals that women face harsher scrutiny than men do with respect to their fiscal and national security credentials. To overcome this disadvantage, Hughes advises women to seek out opportunities to network in those circles by joining trade associations or policy forums that address those issues and to take on sacred cows in business practices and budgets.[15] There will be pushback from entrenched interests who do not appreciate the scrutiny or calls for change, so there is definitely political risk involved. Remember the adage "Sacred cows make the best burgers." Some of the best results come from challenging untouchable issues.

GET YOUR POLICY ACT TOGETHER

All leaders must inspire trust. Before facing the public, you must know what you are talking about.

Research the duties and responsibilities of the position you seek. If you seek a leadership role in a nonprofit, labor union, business association, political campaign, or elective office, con-sider the prerequisites. Does the position require any particular credentials? Do you need a certified public accountant license or a law degree? Do you need ongoing professional education? If so, take care of business. If you are considering working for a gov-ernment agency or elected official, look into the responsibilities to constituents, casework, and staffing requirements. Sit in on public hearings and visualize yourself participating—you may have the requisite patience or you may find that you'd rather be out in the streets than endure long meetings behind a dais.

Master the public policy challenges. As you develop an understanding of the ideological, logistical, budgetary, and practical consequences of your own ideas, be sure to study policy triggers—the events or actions that affect laws. If you are gathering signatures for a ballot initiative, read the proposal first and be sure to understand what the law is now and how your measure will change it. Did you know that many states link some of their tax rates to federal tax rates? Check to see if your state does that before proposing a change in tax policy. One candidate did not check and proposed a federal tax cut that—if passed—would have unbalanced his state budget and left it in deficit. The governor was understandably displeased when called for comment. Another trigger to watch out for is the sunset date of any legislation: you don't want to get caught proposing a budget or law based on a provision that has expired.

Be knowledgeable and candid about the consequences of your proposals. Your word is your bond in politics. People have to trust you as an advocate. As a practical matter, your arguments are stronger if you can identify and counter the strongest arguments against them. As a personal matter, your integrity is underlined by your candor about the merits of your position versus the opposition. The late Jack Valenti—a decorated World War II–combat pilot, Harvard MBA, speechwriter for President Lyndon B. Johnson, and longtime president of the Motion Picture Association of America—cautioned a bipartisan Capitol Hill audience: "Trust is everything." Valenti urged us to be honest about our ideas and candid about our opponents because, he said, the people you are trying to influence will find out the merits of the other side eventually and will respect you all the more for being up front with them.[16]

Think like an innovator. Poll-driven messages are well and good as data points but no substitute for independent thinking. As Clayton M. Christensen has opined, the quest for truth requires an intellectual curiosity to "ask the right questions" if we want fresh proposals to solve vexing problems. In *The Innovator's DNA*, authors Jeff Dyer, Hal Gergersen, and Dr. Christensen build on their idea of disruptive innovation to explain the five discovery skills—the cognitive skill of associating and the behavioral skills of questioning, observing, networking, and experimenting—that constitute what they call the innovator's DNA, or the code for generating innovative business ideas. Their research on roughly five hundred innovators compared to roughly five thousand executives led them to identify these five discovery skills that distinguish innovators from typical executives.[17] Applying innovative thinking to public policy challenges is essential to broaden your circle of policy sources and to bring fresh perspective on old issues.

Balance your purist and pragmatic tendencies. Do you see yourself as a purist or a pragmatist? How much of each? As just discussed, it might depend on the cause. Finding your balance with candor and clarity is essential to your success as people look to you for leadership. A purist can limit alliances or even discussions to like-minded people, but a pragmatist will have to reach across the spectrum of views to talk with everyone. Just as in the DADT repeal debate when progressive Democrats were working with conservative Republicans, the ability to see the humanity in opponents and to compromise on tactics but not principles led the way to transformative change.

See the "kaleidoscope" of politics. It helps to see activism through what Nancy Pelosi calls the "kaleidoscope" of politics. For example, when it comes to the environment, some of the same evangelicals and secular humanists who oppose each other with respect to the separation of church and state agree on the need to combat global warming, while environmentalists and hunters who hold opposing views on gun control share a conservationist agenda to preserve natural resources. You never know where you might find common cause with people, so don't write anyone off and don't wait to get elected—start when you

start running. There must be some point of bipartisan agreement somewhere—be it in seeking lifesaving stem cell research,
veterans benefits, or investing in an innovation agenda. Yes,
there is much polarization now at the national level, but there is
also much agreement among the American people that we must
come together to find solutions.

In the words of former congresswoman Lindy Boggs of Loui-
siana, "Never fight each fight as if it were your last," because
today's adversaries may well become tomorrow's allies. Your
cause is bigger than your ego: no need to fight a scorched-earth
battle only to wake up the next day needing grassroots support
from former opponents for your venture.

"Bush is right." As former Indiana congressman and 9/11 commissioner Tim Roemer counseled, aspiring public servants must
find at least one issue on which to promote bipartisan solutions.[18]
These three words from the first edition of this book drew many
jeers from those who could not find even one reason to like the
former president. But then some of them started quoting Barry
Goldwater on DADT repeal and Nancy Reagan on stem cell
research, and yes, even George W. Bush on funding for AIDS
in Africa, and lo and behold there was a little common ground
after all. No matter how much you disagree with people on the
other side of the philosophical spectrum, there must be at least
one issue on which you can work with the opposition to forge
a constructive solution. Your willingness to communicate the
issues of a shared vision will demonstrate your maturity as a
political thinker and as a public servant. If you are engaged in
electoral politics, your success relies on a bipartisan vision for
America on at least one issue; if you are in the nonprofit world,
your tax-favored status depends on it.

One person who balanced pragmatic and purist tendencies to
great result was Father Robert Drinan, a Catholic priest who
served in Congress and was known as the consummate "pragmatic idealist" because he retained his core values yet moved

★ ★ ★ CALL TO SERVICE ★ ★ ★

FATHER ROBERT F. DRINAN

The ongoing responsibility to public service is embodied in the advice from the late congressman Father Robert F. Drinan to a group of his Georgetown University Law students: "As I look out at all of you with your new and expensive law school educations, I would urge you to go forth into society not as mere legal tradesmen, but as moral architects. Design, create, and build a better and more equitable society, and use your skills to help those who are otherwise not being served."

Drinan agitated for justice for most of his eighty-six years. He was elected to Congress, where he served as chair of the Criminal Justice Subcommittee of the House Judiciary Committee and later opted to remain in the priesthood when the pope asked him to choose between his office and his ordination. Drinan's passion for justice included service in the law school classroom and the nonprofit boardroom, earning his peers' respect, with twenty-two honorary degrees as well as the 2004 American Bar Association Medal and the 2006 Congressional Distinguished Service Award, those institutions' highest honors. His final homily, delivered at the beginning of the 110th Congress in January 2007, was a powerful call to service seeking justice for the children of the world, particularly the children affected by Katrina and Darfur.

Source: Father Robert F. Drinan, remarks at mass honoring Speaker-elect Nancy D'Alesandro Pelosi at Trinity University, Washington, D.C., January 3, 2007. http://www.trinitydc.edu/news_events/2007/012907_fr_drinan.php.

beyond his own ideological circle to find new allies to advance his causes.

Remember: criticism and effectiveness go hand in hand. A classic axiom of public life is, "You can go to church to confess your sins, or you can go into politics and have your opponents confess them for you." Indeed, sometimes your opponents confess sins you never committed and you must confront and debunk them. Chain e-mails and snarky tweets used to gain lives of their own hurtling unchecked through cyberspace before Snopes.com and other debunkers began to offer help in the quest for Truth 2.0.

Campaigns are environments where the stakes are high, the pressure is intense, the media coverage is not always fair or balanced, and the competition is not always decent. Now that everything happens online, everyone from the lead spokes-woman to the newest intern is an ambassador for the cause and subject to relentless public scrutiny. The bigger the stage, the harsher the criticism. Just about anyone who has ever written a blog has been trolled by nasty comments and cyberbullied by people acting like schoolyard jerks. Unfortunately it comes with the territory. The more dedicated you are to your cause, the easier it is to put yourself in the public eye, let the water roll off your back, and keep fighting the good fight.

DECIDE WHICH LEADERSHIP ROLE IS BEST FOR YOU

Take a hard look at what you say about you. In most community organizations, you must complete a background check to serve on a nonprofit board of directors. Be sure that your résumé is accurate, your credentials are sufficient, and you can explain any past mistakes that may come up. Most of all, be sure you have lived up to your code of ethics and the standards by which you judge yourself and others. If you preach family values, live them. If you seek forgiveness for your transgressions, forgive others in personal and public life. Nothing stings more sharply than hypocrisy.

Consider the answers you would owe to your spouse, your children, your friends, your supporters, and the media, should skeletons tumble from your closet. Take an honest inventory of your life now, and review it with your circle of trusted advisers.

No one is perfect, but the past need not set precedence for your behavior going forward. People generally care less about your mistakes and more about your atonement. The American people are forgiving and compassionate. If you can express a lesson learned and earn the trust and support of others—particularly those who may have been aggrieved by your actions—you can put events in perspective and continue with your service.

When you assess candidates, how can you tell whether they risk implosion? You can and should ask these questions before giving support:

★ Are they comfortable in their own skin?

★ Do they seem to coldly prefer humanity to humans?

★ When they make big decisions, do they listen to people or keep their own counsel?

★ Do they seem obsessed with their online friends?

Adapting to fame often comes with a healthy fear of failure as well as a fear of success that causes people to self-sabotage. Fear is human—how that fear is managed is what separates adults from children. There are some signs to watch for in yourself and others to make sure the purpose is to *do* something not *be* something:

★ Boasting or brooding in response to praise or criticism

★ Mistaking political relationships (last-name friends) for personal friendships (first-name friends)

★ Making decisions without consulting a "kitchen cabinet" of close advisers

★ Electronic interdependence that becomes codependence when the roar of the digital crowd drowns out the voice of common sense

★ Arguments or inactivity when a major deadline or event approaches

★ Padding résumé or exaggerating support

Consult your family. Your reputation is not individual; your partner, spouse, children, parents, and close friends will also lose their privacy, possibly against their wishes and regardless of your best-laid plans to protect them. Your family and friends must live with you whether you win or lose. All of this must factor into your decision. Explain your call to service, the nature of your mission, and their roles in any public efforts. Before you embark on this family commitment, reach a family decision. You can dedicate sixteen-hour days to your service mission only if your loved ones support you and are ready to face the cameras themselves. Your loved ones may not support your desire to devote your time, energy, and resources to public service because they will not see you very often during the campaign, which may last a year or two. They may or may not offer you support and campaign with you. Teenagers especially have their own lives and are more likely to act out than grow up on camera. Former Alaska governor Sarah Palin will not be the last vice-presidential nominee with an unwed pregnant teenage daughter, because life happens.

With the economy changing and more two-parent, two-job households, nearly everyone is struggling for family time. As blogs like www.MomsRising.org point out, American families need maternity and paternity leave, open flexible work, health care, and childcare—all of which are scarce in public service campaigns. If you are going to campaign, the hours will not be flexible, the time-outs for family care will be minimal, and the stress levels will be high. For as much as we all talk about quality of life, campaigning does not offer much unless you claim it. Carving out boundaries and honoring them is the hardest part of public life because voters expect you to be on call for them.

If you are working on a campaign or running yourself, be sure to declare up front what family time you need and stick to it. Every day requires grocery shopping, preparing meals, helping with homework, and the more relaxing family activities. All of those activities take time—and money if you must hire someone else to do them for you. Can you afford the childcare necessary to nurture your child at home or to bring your child with you on the road and hire a sitter to entertain her while you campaign? These questions will be aimed at women, but with changing gender roles and family circles, will be asked of men as well. Male parents of small children are starting to be asked the same questions about balancing family life in a dual-income household with small children. Gay families are breaking new ground in this conversation: In 2011 Colorado representative Jared Polis, the first openly gay parent in Congress, took a brief paternity leave to be with his son, and San Francisco supervisor Bevan Dufty became the first openly gay politician to make a television ad with his child, a small girl videotaped riding the bus with dad.[19]

When you serve, your family does too, so be sure they have some of your quality time and not just face time. I say from experience that being home and on the phone or the Web does not count to my toddler and likely not to any family member. Make the effort to maintain traditions like coaching little league, going to church or temple, eating brunch, and attending soccer games and class plays. It makes little sense to run on a platform of helping families if you don't get any time to connect with yours. Experience tells me voters would rather know you have established limits on campaigning due to family duties than that you never see your kids. In my opinion, smarter scheduling can squeeze out more family time. Any job that requires you to have no family life is not worth doing.

If you come from a political family, expect even more scrutiny than another candidate. In my races for Democratic National Committeewoman I have heard the gamut from "Love your mom; I'll give you a chance" to "You show up; I like that" to "Your mom didn't impeach George Bush so I'll never vote for you." All comes with the territory—the bigger the name brand, the harder folks kick the tires.

Consider what others will say about you. People competing for the same job—on a board or for a political office—or those who are opposed to your service mission may link your "minor," "distant," "remote," "forgotten," "childish," "foolish," "rash," "young and irresponsible" acts together in order to gain competitive advantage. The more sacred cows you tackle, the more someone who is threatened by change may want to sideline you. So you must ask the hard questions about yourself.

Your life is an open Facebook. Whenever you are seeking support of others to gain a high-profile position, your opponents can play back everything you have said or done through the *New York Times* or a local blog. As everyone from job applicants to presidential candidates have seen by now, your life is an open Facebook, regardless of your privacy settings. Self-described "hacktivists" are able to break into e-mail, track messages, and leak or republish embarrassing information as disgraced former congressman Chris Lee and Anthony Weiner found out after they sexted pictures of themselves to women who were not their wives. The recent News Corporation phone-hacking scandal, where employees admitted breaking into phone records of politicians and murder victims to find profitable secrets, instructs us that voice mail probably isn't private either.

Be prepared by being honest and keeping a sense of perspective. Anyone involved just to *be* something—to have the title or the ego boost—will internalize the praise and the criticism too deeply to be effective. Consider your personal, financial, political, or criminal background, ranging from every address, job, and position you have held to any civil or criminal proceedings in which you have been involved. Remember the Rule of One—everyone tells someone. A friend told me that he once asked a prominent official about a sensitive matter. "I trust you," the official responded, "but I'm not sure I can trust the person you're going to tell." It's human nature—neither lips nor records stay sealed.

Indeed one of the reasons I started boot camps to give advice up front, as candidates decide whether to run and the people decide whether to support them, was due to an unwelcome October surprise release of a candidate's arrest records. His weaselly response to supporters—"I TOLD you I had convictions"—was cold comfort to those who had thought his convictions were beliefs, not misdemeanors. Of course nowadays people don't wait until October for the surprise—opposition research can be dropped at any time, so a front-end risk analysis is a must. Assume you have no privacy because these days you probably don't.

Assess your own financial risk. Your resources include your own funds and your professional career: you may need to take a leave from your job or curtail your work hours. Can you invest 5 to 10 percent of your disposable income, take out a loan, mortgage your home, give up cable TV, and put thousands of miles on the family car?

Jan Brown described the commitment that she and her husband, Fighting Dem Charlie Brown, made when committing to his campaign for Congress: "We cancelled our cable TV subscription, drove thousands of miles to every community in our rural district, and devoted all our spare time to the campaign so we could call attention to a new direction for the Iraq War, for our son Jeff who is serving, and for all servicemembers and their families." The Browns even spent their 2006 wedding anniversary campaigning at a Nevada City house meeting. "Once we arrived, the campaign manager managed to close the trunk on my right hand," remembers Jan Brown. After bandaging her bleeding hand, Jan went to the party, made the "ask" for donations and volunteers, and tried to avoid shaking hands that night. "An anniversary to remember," she joked.[20] Campaigning is a marathon that takes a personal and financial toll: be sure your family is ready to pay it.

Once you take everything into account and decide to go ahead, you are ready to step onto a public stage. You may decide to lead a nonprofit service agency. You may choose to accept a public trust position as an appointed official—city commissioner, deputy prosecutor, or county administrator. You may decide to chair a ballot initiative campaign. You may assume leadership in a political campaign. You may decide to run for office yourself. Make a decision—and do it.

★ ★ ★

GET REAL:
TAKE THE PUBLIC SERVICE FITNESS TEST

Candidates, prospective supporters, and volunteers should take this to test yourselves or to test those asking you for support for candidacies or nonprofit ventures.

1. What is your vision for the future that calls you to service?

2. What is the bold stroke—your big idea—to achieve your vision?

3. What are the core values that shape your vision and ideas?

4. Whom do you admire in your personal life? Who are your political heroes? Mentors?

5. What have you done for others? List your volunteer history and service on your résumé.

6. Whom have you actively encouraged, supported, or mentored in their paths to public service? List the people who claim you as a mentor. Will they talk to strangers, walk precincts in the rain, sleep on floors, or open their homes for you?

7. What is your personal code of conduct, aka your version of Big Daddy's Rules of the Road?

8. What act of political courage have you taken to achieve your vision? Name your biggest sacrifice or risk.

9. Do you understand what the position demands, and are you prepared to meet those demands?

10. Can you ask thousands of people you don't know to give you a job or give money to your cause?

11. How do you handle crisis and criticism about your personal or political baggage?

12. Is your family ready for you to serve?

13. If you put all your time, energy, and effort into a public service campaign, work your heart out and lose, what then?

TWO

★ ★ ★

Define Your Message

Who are you?

THE WHO

Match these leaders to their campaign slogan:

Barack Obama   (a) Don't Swap Horses in the Middle
                      of the Stream

Abraham Lincoln   (b) Change We Can Believe In

Bill Clinton   (c) Morning Again in America

Nancy Pelosi   (d) Don't Stop Thinking about
                      Tomorrow

Ronald Reagan   (e) A Voice That Will Be Heard

Each of these leaders chose a slogan that in just a few words would answer the question "Who are you?" Notice how each message answers the question and defines the leader:

Barack Obama: (b) I am an antidote to war fatigue and
                       transactional politics.

Abraham Lincoln: (a) I am the commander in chief needed
                       to win the Civil War.

Bill Clinton: (d) I am optimistic and youthful.

Nancy Pelosi: (e) I have the political clout to get
                       things done.

Ronald Reagan: (c) I helped America recover from
                       recession.

Define or be defined. To define yourself you must lead with who you are. If people step onto an elevator with a supporter who is wearing your campaign button, what will the button tell them about who you are?

Take it a step further: what is the elevator pitch for you or your supporter to deliver to back up the button? You have less than a minute for your elevator pitch, and so you need a clear, concise argument promoting your effort, something the other person will think about later. This pitch is the heart of your message, and everyone who supports you should know it by heart and be able to make it under pressure.

Defining a message is just as essential for ballot measures as it is for candidates. In addition, ballot measures will affect turnout and affect candidate messaging, since voters will want to know where a candidate stands on issues.

In states like California, where the ballot initiative process allows just about anything to go before voters, legislative fights often carry over into the ballot box. Legislators pass a health care measure, the governor vetoes it, and the losing side circulates petitions to place it on the state ballot for reconsideration. And so forth.

This process grows tiresome for many voters, who feel as though they are doing what they pay public officials to do.

When you seek a "yes" vote on an initiative, the burden will be on you to lay out the urgency of the situation, the policy implications of the initiative, and the practical consequences of doing nothing. The campaign slogan and elevator pitch must define in simple and direct terms why this race matters: why voters must approve this measure; what exactly the initiative will accomplish for people; and how it achieves the vision, ideas, and values that call you to service.

FRAME YOUR MESSAGE WITH A MESSAGE BOX

Defining your message means articulating your vision, ideas, and values and identifying the behaviors (i.e., code of conduct) that reinforce them. Refining your message means positioning it to persuade people to choose your vision, ideas, and values over those of your competition. People do not make choices in a vacuum: for every good reason you can think of for people to embrace your message, there are equally valid reasons not to. To present your strongest case, you must identify the counterpoint and rebut it. Remember Jack Valenti's advice: the most credible messengers are honest and straightforward about their own weaknesses and their opponents' strengths.

The first step to defining your message is to frame it. Your goal is to define a message that energizes people ready to support you, wins over some people who do not start in your column, and divides the people who are planning to oppose you. Framing your message gives people a way to view you in contrast with your opponent. Voters have preconceived notions about political parties or cultural issues long before a candidate shows up. You have to understand what those notions are and how to discuss them if you are going to win over undecided or skeptical voters.

Try this exercise made famous by the late U.S. senator Paul Wellstone of Minnesota. Draw a simple four-quadrant box to summarize your message with what you say about yourself, what your opponent says about herself, and what you say about each other. (Business consultants call this a 2 × 2 matrix.)

What You Say about You—put your best case forward.

What They Say about Them—put their best case forward.

What You Say about Them—why are you better and/or why are they worse?

What They Say about You—why are they better than you and/or why are you worse?

A message box frames what's at stake in the debate, clarifies what you say, and helps you to play defense. You will anticipate where your opponent will attack you, how you can respond, and how you can move the conversation back to your message.

You must present a clear choice and a definite contrast with your opposition (be it opposition to a person or an issue). A mes-

What You Say about You	What They Say about Them
What You Say about Them	What They Say about You

sage box helps articulate that choice and keeps your campaign disciplined. Every strategic messaging decision you make should be consistent with your message box. Please note: this is a tool to use regularly as the campaign unfolds. What they say about you will change over time, and what you say about them will likely change, too.

Before you begin crafting your message, find out what people are already saying about you and your competitor on the Internet. A Google search for your first and last name (or your opponent's) can turn up thousands of Internet hits with newspaper articles about you, minutes of meetings you have attended, donations you have made, organizations you are in, blog commentaries, family histories, and more. Narrow your search with keywords linked to your first and last name, such as your place of residence, your business, your spouse's name, or even *scandal, bad, corrupt*. Paid searches (the database services of LexisNexis, Dialog, and U.S. Politics) go further, covering national and local publications as well as public records, which can reveal current and previous addresses, your voting record, and any history of liens, bankruptcies, deed transfers, tax records, and mortgage records.

START WITH YOUR CALL TO SERVICE

What You Say about You should express your call to service. Whether you are a candidate for office, a volunteer for a campaign, or a policy advocate, your personal story builds trust between you and your audience. Your call to service—your vision, ideas, and values—captures why you care about people and why people should care about you.

Two recent candidates told their personal stories and public service aspirations as part of their campaign messages:

As a child, Senator Kirsten Gillibrand of New York campaigned with her grandmother, who founded Albany's first women's Democratic club and was a pioneer in the women's rights movement. "As a ten-year-old girl, I would listen to my grandmother discuss issues, and she made a lasting impression on me," Gillibrand said. Now a U.S. senator, she credits her success to her grandmother's mentoring and urges women to get involved via offthesidelines.org.[1]

Congressman Jerry McNerney of California was inspired by his son Michael, who in response to the 9/11 attacks sought and received a commission in the U.S. Air Force. Michael suggested that Jerry serve his country by running for Congress. One of McNerney's mailers depicted a young servicemember on the cover asking, "How do I know that Jerry McNerney will protect veterans?" The response: "Because he's my dad." This message vividly displayed McNerney's call for peace and veterans' rights.

Both Gillibrand's and McNerney's messages express their personal stories, their public service aspiration, and the family members who helped inspire the call.

What You Say about You should also demonstrate your trustworthiness. "It boils down to trust," says communications strategist Jamal Simmons. "At the end of the day when you are alone in that room and nobody can see, the public must believe that you will look out for them."[2]

How will people come to trust you? Because you have taken a political risk, taken the lead on an issue, sacrificed for a cause. You will have a track record: your voter registration, votes, volunteer work, charitable contributions, advocacy for others, and performance in public life, all reinforce your message.

To perform this exercise yourself, start at the very beginning. Let's say your campaign is for a challenger with no government

What You Say about You	What They Say about Them
Youth is a fresh face.	Experience will get things done.

What You Say about Them	What They Say about You
Experience is the system, and the system is broken.	Youth lacks the experience to get anything done.

experience and the opponent's team is supporting an entrenched incumbent. Your message begins with *Youth versus Experience.*

CULTIVATE EXPERTS AND ALLIES TO HELP DELIVER YOUR MESSAGE

"Message is so much more than what you say. People will look at who says it, who corroborates it, what you are doing when you deliver the message, where you are when you deliver the message, and whether you refresh, reinforce, and repeat your message," says California political strategist Mary Hughes. "How you deliver your message conveys whether your leadership is authentic, attached to the community, and reflective of the people."[3]

Some questions to ponder as you seek out allies:

★ Who should say your message?

★ Who should talk about the opponent?

★ Who are your allies cross-training and cross-messaging with you?

★ Who should back up your message once you are under attack?

★ What sorts of strategies will you use as message multipliers?

★ What venues work best to reinforce the message?

★ Which former opponent or unlikely ally can speak best?

Remember the main objective here is to answer the question "Who are you?" Yes, you want to present your self-definition but you must authenticate it with support from allies. This is where having a former opponent in law or business or politics stick up for you is especially helpful because unlikely allies cut through the clutter and make people think differently than "the usual suspects." Your current opposition knows this, so in order to undercut your support she will likely undercut your ambassadors as well.

I saw this firsthand on the campaign trail as message allies were attacked by the opposition. Attacks began with Democratic Party candidates referred to as "Democrat" candidates—"democratic" sounds fair, but "democrat" emphasizes "rat" and is used as an epithet, not an explanation. Then attacks moved to candidates— Democrats in Republican communities were morphed into Ted Kennedy then Bill or Hillary Clinton, now Barack Obama or Nancy Pelosi. Then the attacks became a systematic effort to debrand, defund, and demoralize America's nonpartisan center-left institutions (AFL-CIO, NAACP, Planned Parenthood, and even some veterans groups) in order to undercut their effectiveness as ambassadors by forcing them on the defensive and by forcing Republican legislators to abandon prior support for them. The response by We Are One (www.we-r-1.org) was to bring labor and social justice groups together to organize in solidarity for jobs and justice and to stick up for each other when under attack.

The efforts to undercut Planned Parenthood also yielded a strong defense—and a similar strategy of the ambassadors recruiting their own ambassadors to fight back.

The abortion rights debate is polarized: more and more Democrats self-identify as prochoice and more and more Republicans as antichoice. So in early February 2011, Republicans told conservative religious leaders they wanted to win "the war" on defunding Planned Parenthood, and the politics played out mostly along party lines when the House passed a measure to do so. However, during the Senate floor debate the tide turned. Senator Jon Kyl said that abortions are "well over 90 percent of what Planned Parenthood does" and was proven flat wrong. (The number is 3 percent.) His spokesman said, "That was not intended to be a factual statement." Comedy Central's Stephen Colbert laid into him, using videos and a Twitter hashtag #notintendedtobea factualstatement that shamed Kyl and cut through the clutter.

An unlikely Planned Parenthood ally was conservative media titan Richard Mellon Scaife, whose grandmother had been friends with Margaret Sanger. He wrote an op-ed praising her and defending Planned Parenthood. His conclusion "Republicans Wrong on Planned Parenthood" was all the more powerful coming from a conservative Republican.[4] It took a comedian and a conservative to do it, but a progressive victory was won.

The lesson: even your ambassadors need ambassadors. Moving beyond your base, cultivating allies, and backing them up are essential steps in defining your message.

The 2012 Project's Mary Hughes recommends that new candidates especially need to cultivate experts and allies to help craft and validate their message.[5]

For example, many candidates running for office have not served in the military, yet, as legislators at federal, state, and local levels, they must address issues concerning military families and vets. So if you are a civilian and part of *What You Say about You* is that you support veterans and military families, you must be conversant with key policy challenges and integrate them into your message. You will need to communicate the vision, ideas, and values that will help make tangible change in a variety of areas. To corroborate your message, you need experts and allies. Convene an advisory group featuring all branches of military service and generations of veterans to develop your platform on these issues. Build off your Community Inventory (more about this in chapter 3) and look into prominent veterans in your community, veterans' service organizations, military bases, and veterans' hospitals.

Your advisory group should help you articulate the major challenges, for example:

★ Readiness: current membership in the armed services and status of combat operations around the world

★ Recruiting: military recruiting in communities and on campuses

★ Cost: Pentagon budget and the cost of war

★ Jobs: unemployment challenges and employment discrimination

★ Health care: physical and psychological injuries and treatments

★ Family life: including abuse, divorce, and alcoholism rates

Once you understand the key challenges and the changes in policy that you would support to address them, you can draft and incorporate policy statements into your message, develop a calendar of important dates (starting with Memorial Day and Veterans Day), deliver your message to target groups, and ask members of your advisory group to reinforce the message. When you hold events, repeat your message in your follow-up thank-you to participants and press releases to the public. Make sure you call upon your allies to talk about your opponents and back you up when you are under attack. Repeat, repeat, repeat your message wherever, whenever, and however you can.

RESEARCH TO DEVELOP YOUR MESSAGE

Your arguments are stronger when you identify and counter the arguments against them. To do this you must have competitive intelligence. Research assists with message development, helping to define you and control the campaign dynamic with polling, issue research, press relations, and rapid response.

Conduct ethical research. Many people say they oppose negative campaigning, but it works to expose hypocrisy or misdeeds. So how do you balance the desire to run a positive campaign with the need to educate the public about your opponent or with the need to come clean about yourself?

First, conduct ethical research on yourself and on your opponent. Don't break the law or use information gained illegally. Stick

★ ★ ★ ★ ★ ★ ★ ★ ★ ★ ★

CAMPAIGN PLEDGES AND QUESTIONNAIRES: DESIGN BEFORE YOU SIGN

Craft your message strategy before you sign pledges that put other people's words in your mouth. Otherwise you may end up like Michele Bachmann, who signed a marriage pledge asserting in its preamble that blacks had more stable marriages during slavery.* Although the odious slavery reference was dropped, Americans retained questions as whether fealty to this political pledge would trump the pledge a president makes to the Constitution.

On the economic front, the National Committee to Preserve Social Security and Medicare has a "no cut" pledge it encourages lawmakers to sign, while the Club for Growth has a "no new taxes" pledge signed by dozens of Republicans in Washington.

If you want to make a "no pledge" pledge, which is to say that you will not sign onto other people's agendas, say so at the beginning of the campaign.

Remember the most important pledge is the one you make to the people, not the one an interest group asks you to sign.

*Toby Harnden, "Michele Bachmann signs controversial slavery marriage pact," the *Telegraph*. www.telegraph.co.uk/news/worldnews/republicans/8628717/Michele-Bachmann-signs-controversial-slavery-marriage-pact.html.

to the public record. David Mark, Senior Editor at POLITICO and author of *Going Dirty: The Art of Negative Campaigning* says negative campaigning is "most effective when a candidate's criticisms play into preconceived notions voters already have of their opponents. Charges that come out of left field and aren't substantiated are not usually very effective. But if, say, a first time candidate who has been a businessman in real life is accused of wanting to gut environmental protections, EPA citations against their company tend to bolster the claims against them."[6]

Second, be up front about what you dig up about yourself. Like our candidate with "convictions" from chapter 1 who could have talked about turning his life around, everyone has baggage, but few want to admit it. David Mark advises: "The best response to negative campaigning is to put out damaging information on your own preemptively, particularly early in the campaign."[7]

Any professional campaign will do at least a cursory self-vet on its candidate to find the strongest line of attack for the opposition. Former business executive and 2012 Republican presidential candidate Herman Cain should have done so. Mark observes:

> Cain's campaign was predicated on his can-do business experience and strong communications skills that seemed to resonate with rank-and-file GOP audiences. But in late October 2011 POLITICO reported that while heading the National Restaurant Association in the late 1990s at least two female staffers had complained about his personal conduct. POLITICO gave the Cain campaign ten days to respond to the allegations and when they refused to provide any detailed information a reporter from the news organization confronted the candidate directly outside of a news studio—futilely, it turned out.

Rather than ignoring the journalistic inquiries, the Cain campaign could have used that week and a half to communicate with the National Restaurant Association and get its story straight. Once the story broke, Cain kept changing his response, which, says Mark, "practically invited journalists to dig further into his background." If Cain's staffers had done the research, they could have produced a version most voters would have forgiven. After all, many companies make modest financial payouts over disputes about professional behavior. "Had Cain's campaign leaked the information themselves and preempted POLITICO, the storyline likely would not have lasted longer than a day or two."[8]

On the flip side, don't exaggerate your qualifications. Candidates often are insecure about what they have done and wind up padding their résumés or exaggerating support, claiming education degrees they didn't earn or support they haven't garnered.

For example, one fellow told me that the party should support him for Congress because he had great relationships—in fact, he claimed, he helped talk the incumbent into retiring to make way for a fresh horse in the race. When I asked him whether the congressman would say that publicly about him he hemmed and hawed, and that was pretty much the end of his run.

Third, think long and hard before you release material gained from dirty research tactics. The short-lived presidential campaign of former Minnesota governor Tim Pawlenty stumbled for many reasons, including the perception that his camp fed stories about congresswoman Michele Bachmann's migraine headaches to reporters.

In another example, Connecticut senate candidate Linda McMahon leaked information about attorney general Richard Blumenthal's statements about "serving in Vietnam." This was a valid complaint considering that he served during but not in the Vietnam War. However, McMahon, a former wrestling executive, seemed to be taking a public bow for giving the research to the *New York Times* rather than releasing it herself. This made her look a bit too gleeful and undercut the seriousness of the charge. Better for McMahon to have simply compiled the research and then confronted Blumenthal with a Web ad in a more serious, less triumphant way. The message people took was that McMahon was more of a wrestler than a stateswoman, so her candidacy lost steam and never recovered, even though her opponent was the one with the problem.

The lessons: be clear about how you get your information, report your findings honestly, don't twist the facts, and don't act more like a stuntwoman than a stateswoman.

Document and frequently update your research. You should regularly check newspapers, the Web, radio, and television news coverage. Use RSS feeds, Google alerts, and Twitter searches to maintain contemporaneous updates. To see the details asked of aspiring presidential appointees, check out the federal government's Office of Personnel Management Standard Form 85P: Questionnaire for Public Trust Positions.

Follow your opponents and their staffs on Twitter. You never know what staffers may do to undercut their boss. A spokesman for Mitt Romney, who railed against unnamed Barack Obama supporters for calling his boss "weird," was embarrassed when he was revealed as the author of a fake Twitter account purporting to be authored by the opponent of his other Republican client, Scott Brown. One staffer created headaches for two clients, undercutting both men's claims to be positive campaigners.

Follow the money. You should research campaign contributions to see what interests are funding the opposition. That can become part of your message. "Follow the money," says Green-Dog Campaigns' Dotty LeMieux. "This is the number one rule of politics, and it's fair game for a comparison piece." Sometimes the money is the message, as when a special interest is asserting itself. For example, says LeMieux, a California initiative for a new pipeline sounded like a good idea until the list of contributors appeared. Big development wanted that pipeline for a reason, and it was easily defeated, despite big spending on the other side. "Sometimes the money trail is hard to follow, but it can be your ace in the hole. Sometimes, all you need to do is list the sources of funding for both you and the competition. Tell the voters: 'You be the judge,'" she advises.[9]

Once upon a time, the medium was the message—now, the Supreme Court *Citizens United* decision to increase corporate dollars in campaigns means that in politics, the money is the message.

The philosophy behind the Supreme Court ruling that corporate contributions equal political speech appears to be that special interest money is OK so long as it's accompanied by transparency. But the transparency part of the *Citizens United* equation will only work if we have netizens united to share information,

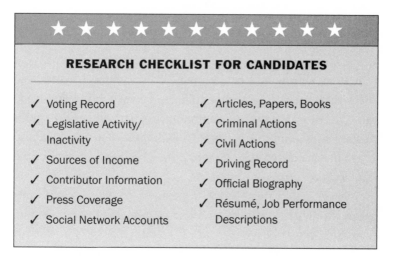

★ ★ ★ ★ ★ ★ ★ ★ ★ ★ ★

RESEARCH CHECKLIST FOR CANDIDATES

✓ Voting Record

✓ Legislative Activity/ Inactivity

✓ Sources of Income

✓ Contributor Information

✓ Press Coverage

✓ Social Network Accounts

✓ Articles, Papers, Books

✓ Criminal Actions

✓ Civil Actions

✓ Driving Record

✓ Official Biography

✓ Résumé, Job Performance Descriptions

track the money, connect the dots between special interests and policy, and enhance new media efforts in campaigns.

Connecting the dots based on online reporting and filings about who is lobbying, who is spending, and who is promising funds won't stop the attacks, but it will condition supporters to know that the hits are coming.[10]

EXPRESS VALUES AND ISSUES

Sierra Club executive chairman Carl Pope advises campaigns to establish a "values bond" with people. "If a candidate talks about values in a way that overlaps with our issues, our people will get excited. For example, 'Ban dirty coal' is a position; 'Promote clean coal' is a values-based agenda. The first one tells people what you are going to do; the second gives us something to do together—it is a values-based agenda that helps build bridges between people."[11]

Campaigns also need to establish "issues bonds" with people. Pope saw polling in which people identified themselves as environment-first voters—their top priority was the environment—and a large percentage of those voters said they were staying home. Why? "The church of politics had disappointed them," reflects Pope. "They needed hope before they would vote." With an environmental initiative on the ballot, the Sierra Club "had to convince them that their vote would matter and that their vote would be counted. So the phone-bankers told them three things: one, this policy will make it the law to do the right thing for the environment; two, we will be at the polls making sure your vote is counted; and, three, don't you want to try to make a difference one more time?" Many of them turned out, and the initiative passed.[12]

You can apply this successful message strategy to any campaign. Establish a values bond and an issues bond before you introduce voters to your political cause or candidate. If your candidate supports cleaning up a polluted river, you could tell environment-first voters that your candidate will prevent people from dumping waste in the river, but they've heard that before. If you show voters your candidate's vision for a clean river and your candidate's alliance with a clean-water group that is making clean rivers a priority, they have a values bond (a shared agenda to clean the river), an issues bond (a shared ally who is actually getting things done for people), and a much better introduction.

CHOOSE YOUR WORDS CAREFULLY

What You Say about You is heard in the context of a larger message environment. You need to personalize your message to reach people how and where they live. Brad Martin, who served as the longtime executive director of the Montana Democratic Party, recalls:

> In Montana, our messaging had not been personal. We were using political jargon, and it wasn't appealing to regular people who don't speak like politicians. So we started to think of our voters as the people who went to our convenience store, where the sign in the window advertises "beer ice ammo" for sale. Rather than direct our remarks to political people, we thought of them as "beer ice ammo" people. We said "general

★ ★ ★ CALL TO SERVICE ★ ★ ★

CARL POPE

Carl Pope's service to protect the environment began over thirty years ago after he performed civil rights work with the Student Non-violent Coordinating Committee in Arkansas and family planning work with the Peace Corps in India. Pope recalls: "Coming home in 1969, I thought of myself as a progressive, not necessarily as an environmentalist. But I came to see that protecting the environment is about what people have in common. Everyone 'owns' the Hudson River, the San Francisco Bay, and Yellowstone. The potential power was organizing for the common good. In 1970 that was true nationally. Now this is true globally: if you drive an SUV today, that may affect a monsoon in ten years. We as a species are not programmed to cope with that."

As the executive chairman of the Sierra Club, Pope sees part of his service as getting people to work together from across the political and economic spectrums to address these challenges. "Politicians need to ask: 'How can we talk about your values and issues in a way that helps you work with other people?' Issue movements like ours spend a lot of time thinking about ways to use our information to build bridges and promote the common good."

Source: Carl Pope, interview, March 27, 2007.

fund" and beer ice ammo people said "Huh?" We switched to balancing the legislature's checkbook and beer ice ammo people responded, "Oh I get it," because no one has a general fund at home but nearly everyone has a checkbook.[13]

Like the Montanans speaking to the "beer ice ammo" crowd you must prepare yourself for how your audience will receive your message, and frame your message accordingly.

Two innovative experts who study the use of language in American politics are Frank Luntz and George Lakoff. During the 1990s Luntz helped change how conservative politicians used words to describe policies. Luntz's Web site identifies his influence: transforming the "estate tax" into the "death tax," "school vouchers" into "opportunity scholarships," and "drilling for oil" into "exploring for energy." Luntz's work demonstrates that powerful words can have a powerful impact.[14] Of course, you must use those words in a message context or frame. For example, "death tax" would not be a successful slogan without the context of the conservatives' ongoing anti-tax messaging.

George Lakoff, author of *Don't Think of an Elephant* (2004) and *Progressive Handbook* (2007), applies a linguist's expertise to politics, urging progressive narratives based on values, ideas, issues, and frames. "First, tell people what you stand for. Tell stories that only make sense relative to your values. For example, I might say that I care about people and want to act responsibly on that care. Government is about protection (our health and safety) and empowerment (our courts and infrastructure)." Thus, you must prepare yourself for how your audience will receive your message and frame your message accordingly.[15]

Luntz and Lakoff impart similar lessons but from different philosophical perspectives: the use of particular words can dictate whether people hear your message as you intend. You won't know until you look behind the words to the values of the people and the context in which they have been expressed.

Choosing your words carefully means incorporating input from your experts and allies. It also means applying common sense. Returning to our Youth versus Experience campaign example, let's say that Youth cultivated experts and allies among other young people, which was great. Then Youth decided to hit hard on the age difference between the two candidates. This was not careful, not smart.

Here's how this situation played out in a recent campaign: A youthful male contender cultivated young allies in his race

What You Say about You	What They Say about Them
Youth can bring new people into the process and is not wedded to old ways.	Experience has a track record.
What You Say about Them	**What They Say about You**
Experience is too old for the job.	Youth attacks old people and will never get anything done.

against an older female incumbent. He said that his alliances could help him get things done for people. He said his opponent could not get things done because she was out of step with the people (fair enough) and because she was too old for the job (big mistake). He did attract new people—to *her* side. At the time, one of her supporters, a woman in her sixties, told me that the challenger was about to find out just how much power so-called old women have to get things done. He did.

On the other hand, if your candidate has been in office awhile and must defend continuity in an anti-incumbent mood, there are ways to present the freshness of your ideas. For example, longtime California Senator Dianne Feinstein has found renewed youth support in taking the lead in a legislative repeal of the Defense of Marriage Act—an effort that has energized a new generation of activists who were schoolchildren during the 1990s culture wars and only recently became voters.

And then there was the spoof the California Democratic party made about Jerry Brown when his opponents criticized him for running for governor in 2010 after having served as governor in the 1970s: Democrats took a highly popular Dos Equis beer ad and played a video montage of Brown through the years. The tagline "Stay Jerry My Friends" used a bit of retro-futurism to present the candidate as political comfort food to a new generation.[16]

Whatever strategy you choose, remember the old adage: Respect your elders. Criticize them for their ideas, not their age.

Defending longtime politicos means offering freshness and confidence, not relying on longevity alone.

USE POLLING TO REFINE YOUR MESSAGE

A winning campaign will spend most of its money to communicate with voters. Polling can tell you what is on voters' minds and how they will hear your message. For example, if you are asserting leadership on a local growth initiative, you will want to determine whether families in the area want new development; whether they want to use taxpayer dollars to fund it; and whether they will give up parkland or wetlands to accommodate new homes, better roads, or additional schools. A simple poll should answer those questions.

Media coverage of political polls usually goes something like this: "Polls show Barack Obama at 50 percent and Mitt Romney at 38 percent, with 12 percent of the voters undecided. The margin of error for the poll is plus or minus 4 percent." These results are called the "horse race numbers," because they simply report who was leading at the moment the poll was conducted.

An early poll is a benchmark that can provide a snapshot of your starting point, particularly in the exploratory phase of a campaign: how well the voters know you or your cause, whether you have traits that the community has never supported—in which case, it's better not to run but to support someone—and what their mood is toward politics and life in general. Later surveys are tracking polls to find out whether and how voters are hearing your campaign message.

Good polls capture more about a race than who are the leaders and laggards; they can help you determine

★ what issues voters believe are most important in an election

★ which voters are most likely to come out and vote

★ what percentage of voters are locked into supporting one candidate or the other

★ what the trends are among the voters and candidates

★ who has momentum

★ whether blocs of voters will move depending on a particular issue

★ if attacked, what responses are needed

★ whether voters are inclined to believe your response to an attack

The two essential candidate questions are "Is America on the right track or wrong track?" and "Who cares about people like me?" Candidates can win by losing one but not both of those. When a candidate happens to be losing on the right track/wrong track question but winning on the "cares about people like me" category, many opponents begin to "other" her—that is, to paint her as different from you and me, far out of the mainstream, and therefore less likely to care about our problems. If your polling telegraphs the othering that is to come, your message box should reflect and refute that.

Think about how you will release your information. Some reporters may want to see the whole poll—not just the good news—before they report on any of it. Laws may require you to release the entire poll if you release some of the poll results. So be careful about disclosing positive results and withholding the negatives. Candor creates credibility. For instance, Stanley Greenberg's Democracy Corps has been praised because it "seeks to measure public attitudes accurately and does not shy away from publishing data that reflects unfavorably on the Democrats." As a laudatory *Democratic Strategist* magazine profile remarked, "The purpose of their research is not to produce politically useful headlines but rather to use the data they collect to guide the comparison and testing of alternative political messages in order to find the ones that most effectively promote a Democratic perspective." That willingness to be brutally honest lends credibility to their advice.[17]

Make sure your polling reaches people where and how they live and who wish to receive information. Traditional polling methods utilized phone numbers from landlines, and so they did not accurately reflect the sentiments of people using cell phones. It is essential to add cell numbers and e-mail addresses to reach people on mobile phones and laptops. Because most young people do not have landlines and barely use e-mail, cell phone contacts are essential, as are peer-to-peer networks and polls of online communities through vendors like SurveyMonkey.

However, just because people use mobile devices does not mean they want your pollsters to contact them that way. I personally am OK with calls or e-mails but not with texts. Others have their own preferences. Be sure your team investigates the various Do Not Call, Do Not E-mail, Do Not Text, and other anti-spam laws before initiating contact and that any costs for answering the call or receiving your text message are covered. This is not just common courtesy—in some venues, it's the law.

If you are trying to get to the heart of voter attitudes, you need in-depth discussions via focus groups and dial groups. Focus groups are small-group conversations with voters about values and issues that can go deeper than your questionnaire. The state-of-the-art technique is to add dial groups, where people listen to a message while at a dial machine that they can crank up, level off, or turn down as they listen. That gives you an even better reading of the elements of your message, and it prevents one person from dominating the conversation as can happen in a focus group.

IF THE FACTS DON'T FIT
THE FRAME, CHANGE THE FRAME

Message framers often use the Albert Einstein adage "When the facts don't fit the theory, change the theory." Apply this to politics and you get this: When the facts don't fit the frame, voters reject the frame. We have two choices—barrage people with statistics that will not change their minds or adopt new frames that change the conversation and move the debate.

For example, when Planned Parenthood was fighting a parental consent ballot measure in California in 2006, the frame was privacy rights versus a parent's right to know. Despite statistics about teen health and safety, some parents were uncomfortable voting to allow their daughters to make intimate choices without them. The organizers talked it through and refined the winning message in the "Think Outside Your Bubble" ad that said, in essence, "You are good parents, so in your world that conversation with your daughter happens, but consider the young women outside your bubble who may have to obtain consent from abusive parents." The frame changed to teen safety versus an abusive parent's right to know, defeating the measure.[18]

INTEGRATE ALL YOUR RESEARCH
INTO YOUR MESSAGE BOX

Let's say your research and polling reveal that people view you as a populist and your opponent as a diplomat, as it did for Paul Wellstone when he ran against Minneapolis Mayor Norm Coleman in 2002. That message box looked like this:

What You Say about You	*What They Say about Them*
Paul is a populist who will fight for people.	Norm is a diplomat who will bring people together.
What You Say about Them	*What They Say about You*
Some fights are necessary; if you get along with everyone like Norm does, you don't make tough choices needed to help people.	If you fight with everyone like Paul does, you can't get anything done.

The voter has a choice: a populist or a diplomat. So rather than just define your message as "I am a populist," refine your message to "We need a populist because some fights are necessary; if you get along with everyone, you aren't making the tough choices needed to help people."

Once you refine your message, use the message box as a guide to your decisions and behavior. For example, once you define yourself as a populist, you have committed to taking on the big fights that come up in the course of your service, such as a large employer in your community that does not pay living wages or provide health care to its employees.

THROW A PUNCH AND TAKE A PUNCH

Campaigns are tough. In the rough and tumble of politics, you have to be prepared, in the words of my grandfather, Thomas D'Alesandro Jr., to "throw a punch and take a punch." *What You Say about Them* and *What They Say about You* are the punches you have to throw and take to compete.

"New candidates are often shocked by the negative campaign ads they've seen on TV and in other campaigns and vow to keep theirs clean and positive," says Dotty LeMieux. She advises people not to be sidetracked by attacks. New candidates fear voters will think less of those who use negative ads, even to defend themselves. They think, "If I get attacked, I'll just explain the truth. The voters will understand." They won't. LeMieux says candidates should use opposition research to make pointed comparisons showing the opponent's negatives. "If you're attacked, you need to quickly respond, and then get back to your message."[19]

In 2002 Georgia Senator Max Cleland lost his seat after his opponent ran ads comparing him to Osama bin Laden. He said,

> The biggest mistake I think we made in 2002 and 2004 is that we let the accusations of the Swift Boat Veterans for Truth [that John Kerry did not earn his medals and was not a war hero] linger too long in the media. We should have swiftly responded back as soon as the attacks appeared on the front page, and instead we underestimated the damage they caused. All future candidates should take that lesson in campaigns when they are attacked with lies and garbage.[20]

Senator Cleland helped lead the movement to establish a Democratic National Committee (DNC) Veterans and Military Families Council; campaigned for dozens of the Fighting Dems running for Congress in 2006, 2008, and 2010; and speaks out quickly against attacks on his allies. By validating Democrats' credibility on national security issues, Cleland enhances the *What You Say about You* element of the message; by pushing back against "swiftboating" attacks, Cleland adds the *What You Say about Them* counterpunch to the debate. Hence, all four corners of the argument are engaged.

Since then, other networks have formed to engage in this space. Dr. Rachel Kleinfeld created the Truman National Security Project, a start-up that now has a $4 million budget to articulate progressive security values, fight for them on the campaign trail, and enact them in government policy. As Kleinfeld explained,

> By 2004, I saw how conservative security policies were making America less safe—and the world less secure. But progressives were in a deep hole with the American public, after forty years of conservatives calling progressive security ideas weak. Growing up in a conservative household, I knew how their leadership training institutes worked—and how effective they were at functioning across silos in policy, electoral politics, and the media. We created the Truman Project to train a new generation of progressive leaders, so we could own this security space again.[21]

USE AGGRESSIVE SCHEDULING TO ADVANCE YOUR MESSAGE

Prioritize every action according to your message. Ask: How does this event help advance the message of the campaign? Why am I here? What votes are here? How does this event help me advance my message? Who will be impressed by my decision to attend or offended by my decision to send one of my allies as a surrogate?

Be consistent. Every event should be consistent with your message. If you say you are a populist but you are only delivering speeches in venues that cost money to attend, you are undermining your own message. On the other hand, don't go overboard and deliver your support-the-troops message in a tank. Keep it real.

Create events that help the campaign advance your message. Anyone should be able to look at the campaign slogan and the calendar and immediately understand the connection between message and event. To take our veterans example, if you are campaigning in support of veterans and military families, you should deliver your message with members of your advisory group on veterans and military families at a house meeting or a town hall meeting, with members of a veterans service organization in attendance.

Refresh, reinforce, and repeat your message. Participate in an online chat or radio interview after a meeting, send the message out to your e-mail lists of supporters and media contacts, and repeat it.

Consult your message box in schedule conflicts. On concurrent events, staff may be evenly divided about which event gets priority. No one will want to compromise. So which event goes on the schedule? Whichever event best advances your message.

Insist that only the scheduler puts events on the calendar. Otherwise, there will be chaos. Schedulers are message managers. They must process dozens of requests and track a million details. A well-organized scheduler will confirm or deny all requests officially. Detailed information is needed on each event accepted, including the exact time the event starts, who will attend, who will speak, and how the message will be advanced through press coverage of the event. Using free cloud computing tools like Google Docs, schedulers can host events and accept virtual responses.

Plan for effect not volume. I worked for Andrew Cuomo when he was Secretary of Housing and Urban Development in the Clinton-Gore administration. He would often look at the schedule with a view toward what we could accomplish well, not how many events we could cram into the calendar. He looked over one particularly ambitious trip proposal and asked, "Are your scheduling eyes bigger than your logistical stomach?" Now New York governor, Cuomo scheduled only in-state events his first year and posted his schedule online to keep his People First campaign pledge.

A good scheduler shows compassion for the campaign team and allows time for food, sleep, exercise, and worship. Without a minimum of rest and reflection, no one performs well. Better to identify fewer events and do them well than to overbook and underperform.

PREPARE TO SEND YOUR FIRST MESSAGE

The first message that a twenty-first-century campaign sends is usually an e-mail announcing a campaign with a link to a Web site. The person sending that e-mail is the campaign's first ambassador. Therefore, from the start it is essential to establish protocols for every ambassador, beginning with Internet use. Nothing instills more confidence than a welcoming Web site or doubt more quickly than an egregiously inappropriate e-mail.

Welcome with your Web site. Your Web site is the public's first exposure to your campaign. It should welcome people to your cause and reflect the vision, ideas, and values of your public service mission. It should encourage visitors to volunteer, contribute, and network. Be scrupulous with any personal data you gather: do not share information with anyone except appropriate campaign finance reporting entities, and never sell it to anyone. Be sure that your information technology vendor understands your ethics. Avoid spyware technology that may violate the privacy of visitors. Constantly update security and check for viruses. People are trusting you with their information and will expect you to allow them to "opt out" of any communications.

Beware of inappropriate e-mails, posts, and tweets. No medium is more permissive and less forgiving than the Internet. Blogging, texting, or tweeting is like getting a tattoo: you want to express yourself in the moment but have it wear well over time because it will be there forever.

Netiquette—the etiquette of using the Internet—is essential to any twenty-first-century public service effort. Here are a few basic rules of netiquette:

1. If you wouldn't say it or post a picture of it off-line, DON'T say it or post it online.

2. DON'T forward other people's messages without their permission.

3. DO assume that other people will forward your message without your permission.

4. DO save copies of important messages and posted items for backup and verification.

5. If you get a group message rather than a blind copy, DON'T harvest it for contact information.

6. If someone calls you on a netiquette lapse, DO apologize in real time and move on.

7. DON'T forget that www stands for World Wide Web— there is no "private" messaging!

Your Twitter followers are not your confidantes; your Facebook friends are not your confessors; your e-mail list subscribers are not your counselors—they are all people with whom you are having public communications. When you need confidantes, confessors, and counselors, pick up the phone—or better yet, meet in person.

Be sure to keep your social networking accounts clear of racist, sexist, homophobic, or otherwise insulting commentary that undermines your code of civility. While you can't track each and every message in a large campaign, monitor sites for vitriol and keep people engaged in spirited but respectful discourse.

Ignore these rules of netiquette at your peril. Florida GOP Congressman Mark Foley went into rehab after media publication of his e-mails to a sixteen-year-old former Capitol Hill page.[22] In New York, Kathy Hochul has Chris Lee's old job and Bob Turner has Anthony Weiner's. Apart from inappropriate conduct, Foley, Lee, and Weiner forgot a fundamental rule: the *e* in *electronic* can also stand for *evidence*. Oversharing ends careers.

★ ★ ★

GET REAL: DRAW YOUR MESSAGE BOX

Create a message box for your campaign. Here's what to put in the box and what each one means:

What You Say about You—Put your best case forward.

What They Say about Them—Put their best case forward.

What You Say about Them—Why are you better/why are they worse?

What They Say about You—Their best case against you/why are they better than you?

What You Say about You	What They Say about Them
What You Say about Them	What They Say about You

Integrate your call to service, allies, research, and common sense into your message box.

★ Who are your allies, alumni, and ambassadors, and which ones best speak for you?

★ What new media strategies will you use as message
  multipliers?

★ How does your schedule advance your message?

★ What venues reinforce the message?

★ How many volunteers can help you?

★ How do your Web site and electronic communications
  reinforce your message?

★ What human technology and coalition networks do you
  have to reinforce and repeat this message?

★ Who is spending money for or against you? What does that
  say about the message?

★ What mobilization metrics do you have to test your message (letters sent, petitions signed, calls made, doors
  knocked, media points, new media connections)?

PART II

MANAGEMENT

THREE

★ ★ ★

Know Your Community

You gotta' know the territory.

THE MUSIC MAN

The traveling salesmen in Meredith Wilson's musical *The Music Man* could be talking about nearly any neighborhood in America: every community has its unique way of life, a political and cultural history that you need to learn in order to serve effectively. You must know your neighbors and their families: How do they live, work, worship, and play? What are their hopes, dreams, and aspirations for their kids and their parents? In short, you gotta' know the territory.

As you look to serve your community as a volunteer for a cause or as a candidate for office, prepare, connect, and target: prepare a Community Inventory, connect with leaders, and target supporters. First, prepare a Community Inventory by gathering raw data about your community's *people, economy, geography, traditions, opinion leaders, politics, social networks,* and *challenges.* Second, connect with the community leaders, organizations, and networks that enhance civic life. Third, target people who are likely to support your candidate or cause.

Look at whether significant races (such as the presidential race or ballot initiatives) or highly competitive local races will be on the ballot because these contests historically bring more voters to the polls. As discussed in chapter 2, it is important to know what is on the ballot so you get a flavor for where your candidate or cause fits within the message environment.

PREPARE A COMMUNITY INVENTORY

There is no substitute for crunching the numbers and filling in the local wisdom so you know the territory. You might want to have volunteers or staff each take on a piece of the Community Inventory then compare notes to put a composite together. In my UC Extension Public Service Leadership Boot Camp class, for example, we divided up the San Francisco Bay Area among students who each conducted a Community Inventory on a particular element. Then we compiled our notes to build a matrix. Having a sense of place gives you a sense of purpose. Let your Community Inventory be your guide.

Know the people. Begin with the people in the community. Look up the national census data, employment data, and local sources of demographic data to show the people in terms of age, gender, ethnicity, and family units.

Then look at how people live: Do they rent or own their homes? What is the per capita income? How does the per capita income vary by neighborhood? Where do the children, young people, and adults go to elementary school, college, or vocational school?

Know the economy. List the top ten employers in the private, public, and nonprofit sectors and the five fastest growing small business opportunities. List the national security infrastructure, be it a military base, defense contractor, or veterans hospital. Identify which unions work which jobs. List schools and universities. Identify the first responders. Look up this information online and gather it in conversation with local and ethnic chambers of commerce and labor unions. You will expand your knowledge base and your networks.

Know the geography. Map your community, be it urban, suburban, rural, or a combination. "Maps tell you about the territory," says 2012 Project's Mary Hughes. She encourages aspiring public servants to collect as many maps as possible of parkland, transit routes, political districts, schools, population and growth centers, real estate (such as available commercial space), historical museums and landmarks, and critical infrastructure. "You don't know your community until you know these basics," Hughes advises.[1]

Think of it this way: What is on the postcards? In the local history books? When disaster strikes, what physical icons matter most? These are places where you should be campaigning and connecting. Incumbents, do yourself a favor—don't stand in front of a capitol or city hall dome when you campaign—stand in front of one of these landmarks instead and tell people what you did to maintain the values it reflects.

Know the traditions. Every community has traditions that shape the local culture: the Big Game, annual neighborhood or ethnic festivals, Fourth of July parades, chamber picnics, beach clean-ups, walkathons, and 5K races. Each of these events requires the support of community leaders—block club presidents, church deacons, shop stewards, and parent-teacher association (PTA) officers—who bring people together to participate. For example, PTA officers have been networking for years with other parents and teachers, so they have their fingers on the pulse of the community.

There is an adage about Boston that its favorite traditions are "politics, sports, and revenge." Anyone who has seen political coverage of John Kerry, Mitt Romney, or the Boston Red Sox knows that the reputation is only partially tongue-in-cheek: the press is pretty tough and the players must be too. Few Bostonians will forget the woes of Martha Coakley, an effective attorney general but ineffective campaigner whose gaffe of mistaking a Red Sox hero for a Yankee fan is a cautionary tale for the ages. People who love their traditions will expect you to love them too, or at least to do your research before venturing to comment on them.

As a practical matter, you want to work with, not conflict with, community events. It is a lot cheaper to set up a booth at one of these events than it is to establish your own event altogether, so your scheduler should keep these traditional events on your calendar so that you can use them to create message opportunities—like a team in the local 5K run—or avoid obvious conflicts like phone-banking in the middle of a big game.

Know the opinion leaders. Every community has its icons: people who command respect through their outstanding achievement in political, business, cultural, or philanthropic endeavors: newspaper columnists, labor leaders, corporate executives, nonprofit directors, civil rights and human rights activists, city or county commissioners, and people connected with cultural landmarks, places of worship, and highly regarded institutions, such as universities, policy think tanks, foundations, civic organizations, chambers of commerce, and other business associations.

Author Malcolm Gladwell differentiates among opinion leaders as connectors, mavens, and salesmen from the community. His book *The Tipping Point* explains: "Connectors are individuals who have ties in many different realms and act as conduits between them, helping to engender connections, relationships, and 'cross-fertilization' that otherwise might not have ever occurred. Mavens are people who have a strong compulsion to help other consumers by helping them make informed decisions. Salesmen are people whose unusual charisma allows them to be extremely persuasive in inducing others' buying decisions and behaviors." Gladwell identifies a number of examples of past trends and events that hinged on the influence and involvement of connectors, mavens, and salesmen at key moments in their development.[2] Apply this thinking to your work.

Through local news outlets and online searches, you can identify these connectors, mavens, and salespeople. Divide your search into major categories: tech, education, arts, disease research, children, civil rights, and so forth. Search the Web to see the incidences of appearances of connectors, mavens, and salespeople in the news to determine who is most often quoted. Then "friend" or "follow" them to see why and to track their networks. Chances are they are saying something you need to know.

Know the politics. Who are the voters? Look at how people vote: how many are eligible, registered, and voting? Get voter registration figures and election results from your secretary of state or county elections official to see how many people registered and voted in recent elections. Check the census to see how many young people will be of voting age by Election Day. What election technology does the community use, and do citizens vote early, by absentee ballot, or by mail? If most people vote early, for example, you might begin your outreach earlier and develop an early-voting campaign strategy. Looking up the voting patterns also means looking at the fights to restrict or expand voting rights. Many restrictions are being passed as I write this book, so make sure your information is current. Rock the Vote's Web site has good indices of voting laws, so check there and with your local election protection experts.

Look at the incumbents: the people elected at the local, county, state, and federal levels. What do they say about themselves? Visit their Web sites, read their blogs, see who follows them on Twitter, and research news archives for text, audio, and video. This research will also provide good information for your message box.

To be effective, you need the support of others who have served before you. Review your relationships with the people elected to represent your community at the local, county, state, and federal levels. Consider also the various political camps in your community, and who is on which side. Will you be forced to choose sides? If so, which side shares your values? Have you worked for or against the election of any of these people? Did everyone come together after the last fight, or do you have some fence mending to do? Which of these elected officials and political leaders are likely to get involved in your cause or campaign?

Party registration data will give you an idea as to whether people tend to vote for members of your party. Independent voters in states that allow party registration have already made a decision: they have opted not to register with a particular political party.

Political party registrations give you a starting point, but you have to look beyond party labels to discern voters' concerns. Check election results for ballot initiatives relating to taxes, growth, school bonds, library bonds, labor relations, and social issues because they may reveal voters' values and the priorities that those values represent. After a review of the voting patterns, consider whether there is a deciding voting bloc that can determine the outcome of the election. If the numbers are not in your favor, consider whether you have the resources to register enough new voters or persuade enough voters to cross party lines to support you or your candidate.

Know the social networks. Members of most communities hang out in both physical and virtual spaces. The August 26, 2011 Pew Internet and American Life Survey calculated that 50 percent of Americans are online, and 66 percent of online adults use social media platforms.[3] So you will need to include peer-to-peer social networking in all your outreach.Find out where your voters spend their time online, and get to know each audience.

"They all have different focuses, different cultures, and different personalities. One blog or community is not like any other," says *Daily Kos* founder Markos Moulitsas.[4] "Know whether a site's culture revolves around a high-profile lead blogger, or whether it's a more community-minded approach," advises Moulitsas.

For example, members of the *Daily Kos* community organized a national convention—Yearly Kos—that morphed into

Netroots Nation. True to the spirit of *Daily Kos*, the Netroots Nation activities include crowd-sourced agenda items, cross-trainings by various progressive stakeholders, and "Netroots for the Troops," a volunteer service activity.

Know the challenges. Gerald W. McEntee, president of AFSCME, expects aspiring leaders to know "the hopes and the challenges of the people in your community. More than being aware of problems, you need to care about people's challenges and have a way to help solve them," he says.[5]

Economic challenges, for example, manifest themselves in ways unique to your community. For some communities it may be underwater home mortgages in a slumping housing market; for others, a "brain drain" as kids who leave for college do not come home to work and raise families; and for still others, a more industry- or company-specific challenge. When my UC Extension class prepared a San Francisco Bay Area Community Inventory in 2010, at the beginning of the semester we listed the NUMMI auto plant in Fremont, California, as among the largest employers. A few months later, the plant was closed, meaning a loss of jobs to the thousands of workers at NUMMI and at companies supplying car parts, as well as a loss to the community of consumer and philanthropic dollars. We could chart the ripple effects of the plant closing across the community. When plans were announced to reopen the plant via Tesla Motors several weeks later, the people's economic prospects and our Community Inventory changed again.

NETWORK WITH GROUPS AND COMMUNITY SERVICE LEADERS

Now that you have mapped out the territory, you can engage with the various networks relevant to your campaign or candidate.

If you are thinking of running for office or accepting a leadership position with a community-wide nonprofit agency, get out

★ ★ ★ CALL TO SERVICE ★ ★ ★

GERALD McENTEE

For Gerald McEntee, union organizing began in the family. His father was a garbage truck driver in Philadelphia, who rose to be a union steward, business agent, and head of the local council before being elected vice president of AFSCME. McEntee's childhood memories include his dad on the phone all night listening to grievances and trying to solve problems. After serving in the army, McEntee went to work as an organizer and led a campaign to attain collective bargaining rights in Pennsylvania. He rose to head the state union and then served as his father had as international vice president of AFSCME before being elected president of the union and its 1.4 million public service employees.

What continues to motivate McEntee after fifty years in the public service employee union and over twenty-five as its president? It is the unfinished business of helping working families. On Labor Day 2011 McEntee said,   ▶

and visit. If you are running for office or organizing a public service mission, begin with a listening tour, where you can meet people and hear the community's concerns.

No one expects you to make up for a lifetime in a few months; however, people do expect that if you are going to lead, you will begin by showing your respect for them. Explore, don't exploit. Nothing alienates potential allies faster than blanket requests for support or cash. Observe before participating. Failing to listen or to respect a community's protocols is a pet peeve of community leaders, online and off. Sometimes you need an invitation; you cannot just show up. Like in-person meetings with members, online communities are platforms for conversations, not for self-promotion. "If you want to come and have a chat, then most online communities will give you a fair hearing. If you come in

> ▶   Now, more than at any time in recent years, workers are aware
> of how the deck has been stacked against them. Yet the focus of
> too many politicians has not been on pulling together to find real
> solutions or creating good jobs or helping working middle class
> families hold on to their homes and their dreams for the future.
> Instead, they are giving even more power to the greedy interests
> who created the worst economic crisis since the Great Depression.
> This Labor Day, we are sending the powerful CEOs and their politi-
> cal allies a new message: "We are prepared to fight for the future."
>
> AFSCME established candidate boot camps because members
> are concerned about many issues. McEntee explains, "We want to
> make sure candidates are prepared to address them with honesty,
> vision, a mind and a heart that automatically go to the problems
> of working people, and a plan to win." McEntee is still inspired by
> memories of his father on the phone working out problems and
> expects public officials to do the same for their people: "to be aware
> of the existence of problems in their district, to have a bond with
> people, and to work toward solutions."
>
> *Source:* Gerald McEntee and Lee Saunders, September 5, 2011.

trying to market to them, they'll turn on you with a vengeance,"
says Moulitsas. "Realize that you aren't the only person, campaign, or operation with an important mission. Give people a
reason to get excited about your efforts and don't assume or
expect anything."[6]

Friend-raising should come before fund-raising. Make friends
by providing information (friend-raising) before requesting contributions (fund-raising). Democratic netroots guru Tim Tagaris
advises candidates to (1) communicate directly with communities, (2) involve netroots in your effort, (3) reach out to opinion
leaders, and (4) position yourself on the issues, relative to your
opponent. He says, "The ideas of 50,000 [people] will almost
always be better than the ideas of five people who live their
entire lives inside of a campaign headquarters."[7]

You must prepare to cede control and listen to the wisdom of crowds if you are to represent people or attract them to your cause.

Congressman Bruce Braley's work in Iowa's First Congressional District is instructive. When Braley first ran, this was an open seat with no incumbent and no clear advantage in voter registration for either political party. Braley made a commitment to represent everyone in the district, no matter their political party, and set out to visit with as many people as possible. Braley posted a map of all twelve counties on his Web site so people could click on the county for a schedule of events, which included meet-and-greets, town hall forums, pork chop dinners, 5K runs, and homecoming parades. By the time his tour was finished, Braley had a deeper respect for the traditions and a broader knowledge of the values and issues in the campaign. The people, in turn, had his visits to their neighborhoods and his articulation of their issues as proof that he saw them as his future employers.[8] Now five years into the job, Braley continues to tour his district, revisiting all those areas and, in recent months, laying sandbags and offering assistance to the areas savaged by flooding, all the while Tweeting his perspectives to followers.

Like Congressman Braley, you must get out and visit with people in order to understand their aspirations. Be sure to keep in contact with the people you meet, adding them to your various networks as appropriate. Ongoing updates will let you know what issues are most on people's minds as well as the fundraising and organizational work they are doing.

Few people knock on 25,000 doors through their entire volunteer operation, so that perseverance helps explain why Debbie Wasserman Schultz won her first election for the Florida legislature with 64 percent of the vote.[9] Her husband made her milkshakes to keep up her strength, and off she went to meet the neighbors one household at a time. She went on to congress and became the first woman nominated to chair a major political party by a sitting president. As the congresswoman has reminded candidates at our AFSCME boot camps, knocking on doors gave her the best polling data possible: direct feedback from the people.

If you are working with an incumbent, keep visiting with people as aggressively as you did when the person was a candidate first seeking the job. By all means, don't stop listening. Many newly elected party and public officials embark on thank-you tours when they are elected and listening sessions once they are in office to stay close.

If you've lost and are trying for a comeback, make sure you show growth and not a grudge. Congressman John Tierney of Massachusetts ran three times against the same opponent, losing in 1994 and winning in 1996 and 1998. "Anger doesn't work," cautions Tierney. "Better to identify what people liked in your campaign and highlight and improve on that." Tierney advises repeat challengers: "Do not run the last campaign. Essentially, it is all about keeping your base from the last time and building a new voter group through concentrated outreach."[10]

If you are working for a public servant or are an incumbent yourself, help the other members of your community's official family. Congressman Mike Thompson, Democrat of California, a leader of the Blue Dog Coalition, advises you to stay close to your family of elected officials. Thompson cooks up an annual pasta feed hosting all the elected officials and community leaders in each county of his sprawling north coast California congressional district.[11]

Use social media to organize local groups and individuals for fact-finding, fund-raising, and communicating with the public. Once you build your networks, be sure to find ways to keep them going—even after you win. Now that the economy is sputtering and the Tea Party has urged Republicans not to spend money on direct stimulus investments, the Obama administration faces the task of re-engaging those networks and re-enlisting support. One lesson they learned the hard way was not to let their network atrophy. Their e-mail list of 11 million people withered on the vine for several months before becoming engaged for the health-care debate several months into the administration. Though its revival certainly helped pass health-care reform, the relative inaction in the early months of 2009 undercut the president's support among his base. Going forward, the lesson for President Obama and for any elected official is to keep that network going because there is only a limited opportunity to make change. Winning only matters if you can translate it into making progress in people's lives.

Build coalitions. Look for unlikely allies to join your networks. GreenDog Campaigns' Dotty LeMieux (introduced in chapter 1), described a coalition to require that any new construction at the Marin County Civic Center be subject to a public vote. "A preservationist group attracted the interest of prison reformers (because a new jail was being contemplated at the site), anti-tax advocates (who feared they would have to foot the bill for some lavish building projects), and neighbors (who wanted to keep things quiet)," she recalls. LeMieux and her unlikely allies sought endorsements from conservationist groups like the Sierra Club and social justice networks whose members joined their ranks as volunteer precinct workers, phone-bankers, and donors.[12]

Similarly, when plans surfaced for a biotech medical research facility on one of the most visible hillsides in Marin County, these same groups formed a coalition. According to LeMieux, a referendum opposing the facility passed easily with the support of animal rights activists (who were against animal testing) and local service providers (who were against new competition for resources). Conversely, an effort to stop a new golf course on the site of a historic blue oak forest failed because the developers offered discount greens fees to local golfers, who outnumbered the environmentalists.

Create affinity groups. Most national organizations have local leaders who have engaged in various political and community campaigns. Whether you are looking to Occupy, MoveOn, or have a Tea Party, you can visit the sites and enter your zip code to find events in your community. These organizations often form coalition networks around particular issues such as income inequality, Constitutional rights, education, energy, taxes, and net neutrality.

Tap into campus networks. Outreach to and input from young people are especially critical. Nearly every community has a college, and nearly every college has a tradition of student activism, including local chapters of national organizations. Many of these organizations have years of experience in developing young leadership.

If you are seeking progressive volunteers, look for Young Democrats of America, College Democrats, progressive campus networks devoted to women's rights or the environment, Public Interest Research Group (PIRG), ethnic organizations, and lesbian, gay, bisexual, and transgender (LGBT) pride chapters. If you seek conservative volunteers, look for local chapters of College Republicans or conservative campus networks such as the Intercollegiate Studies Institute (ISI), the Collegiate Network, the Leadership Institute, Young America's Foundation, or the Heritage Foundation.

Consider groups that reach across the political spectrum to organize around causes. For example, young Americans from a variety of political and religious traditions are asserting leadership on the cause of combating genocide in the Sudan. Web sites like SaveDarfur.org and RocktheVote.org list local Divest for Darfur chapters. Log on to see if there are any chapters in your area.

Outreach to college students should start where they are and start when they start. Have a plan for the week before classes start. Staff a table the first two weeks of classes every semester. Recruit young people to provide feedback and to lead the effort, give them training, help them write a plan, and coach them to be competent civic activists.

Empower youth networks. Effective outreach finds youth where they are—on the Web, via text messaging—addresses and produces on the issues they care about, and approaches them in an authentic style. Pollster Celinda Lake expects young voters to be a battleground constituency in 2012. "Research demonstrates that people who vote the same way three times in a row tend to vote that way disproportionately over the rest of their lifetime."[13] With young people having voted for Democrats in 2006, 2008, and 2010, anticipate that Democrats will try to seal the deal in 2012, while Republicans will try to break the pattern.

A dynamic youth network is the Bus Project in Oregon. Founder Jefferson Smith and director Matt Singer combine humor and activism to engage young people.[14] In 2004, organizers coalesced around a strategy to get a bus, put young people on the road, and drive into competitive districts to talk to voters. By 2010, their Trick or Vote program had thousands of volunteers in over seventy-five cities dressed up in costume to talk to over 200,000 people, reminding them to vote. Their viral videos of kids dressed up in costume asking people to vote remind me of my own childhood. What began in Oregon has spread to several states, and even to the country of Cameroon.

Connect with seniors networks. The fight over Social Security, Medicare, and Medicaid will dominate elections as millions of seniors press for the hard-earned benefits that others wish to cut. Mess with the safety net at your peril. Nancy D'Alesandro, my maternal grandmother, who led her "Moccasin Army" of ladies in Baltimore politics, once said in a fight with the power company: "I'm on a limited income with unlimited time." Connect with the senior centers and networks in your community, remembering that they are the least likely to be online. Some, like the National Committee to Preserve Social Security and Medicare, are online and tweeting @NCPSSM, but most remain off-line or without cell phones. So text messaging is statistically not the way to reach them.

The seniors networks will kick-start your messaging on Social Security, Medicare, and Medicaid, but remember these issues are intergenerational, so be sure your messaging includes all layers. Saving Social Security is also a priority for women aged 45–65. Celinda Lake elaborates: "Women aged 45–65 tell us in focus groups 'Social Security is all we have. We are already raiding retirement to help our kids.'"[15] Young people are concerned about Medicaid because for many it is the source of health-care funding. Contacting the senior in a multigenerational household, therefore, will not "cover" the issue. You need networks to do that. A good example is the Sarah Silverman Get Bubbe to Vote ad in 2008. By convincing young people to get their grandparents to vote, she engaged in an intergenerational effort with humor.

If you are running for office, include your primary foes in your coalitions. After a primary, it is essential that your team present a united front. One of my rules for baseball is, "Don't boo the home team." That's what the other side is for. Remember President Ronald Reagan's eleventh commandment: "Thou shalt not speak ill of another Republican."[16]

Montana Democrats created their own version of the eleventh commandment: Don't make other people pay the price for our divisions. Brad Martin remembers: "We constantly reminded ourselves that other people paid the price of our divisions. When a poor child did not get health care or a hot meal because we were fighting each other, and losing elections, that child paid the price." Martin recommends building a coalition network including your former foes by giving thanks and reaching out: "Thank your supporters. Reach out to your primary opponents and their supporters. You won. Be gracious."[17]

I once walked precincts for a candidate who had not cleaned up an internal political fight from years before. It was a real problem with some members of his community who wanted him to reconcile with his foe before they would give this candidate a promotion. He didn't, and they didn't.

TARGET YOUR SUPPORTERS

To determine whether your cause or candidate can succeed, take a look at different groups of people and target the folks whose support you need.

Software programs will allow you to create categories of information and merge them into a master file. For party committees, candidates, and ballot initiative campaigns it's Voter Vault or VAN technology: voter files purchased from election officials and updated with consumer data. Nonprofits have lists of names, addresses, phone numbers, e-mail addresses, and participation histories. Voter files are essentially the same—public Rolodexes telling you who registered, whether they registered with a political party, where they live, and how often they vote. (It may also have e-mail addresses and telephone numbers.) Voters are organized by small geographical units covering a few city blocks or county roads called *precincts*, which include about a thousand voters according to a the U.S. Election Assistance Commission.

How do you use these tools?

* Take this list of voters in each precinct of the area you want to cover.
* Crosscheck it with your Community Inventory data—people, geography, traditions, leaders, politics, and networks.
* Merge the file with commercially available consumer information, personal Rolodexes, membership lists, and input from individual volunteers who have reached these voters directly.

Let's say you are organizing support for a ballot initiative to promote after-school programs. One approach is to reach out to the PTA officers and child advocacy groups in your community and invite people to share their personal Rolodexes and organizational membership lists so you have a list of potential allies to identify. Then crosscheck these names against the voter files in your precincts to see who registered and votes, who should update their registration, and who needs to register.

Once you identify potential supporters, the people making peer-to-peer contact can ask for support and provide specific information on where to register. If voters express support for your cause or candidate, update your file. If allies register to vote or update their registration, update your file and ask the registrar of voters to provide you with an updated list.

National party committees use databases to identify voters with labels showing what issues would likely persuade them to vote Democratic or Republican so that people can call or visit these voters to encourage them to vote. Longtime Republican presidential adviser Karl Rove has trumpeted "microtargeting": using databases and search tools to divide voters by their backgrounds and interests, appeal to them with tailored pitches, identify sympathetic voters, and try to move them to the polls.

During the 1987 Nancy Pelosi for Congress campaign, we deployed the Nana Brigade—my paternal grandmother and her friends sending postcards to their neighbors with Italian surnames urging them to vote. I recommend that every campaign establish a Nana Brigade of sorts—friends and family reaching out to their networks. Nowadays, the Nana Brigade meets Karl Rove. Rather than have nanas highlight names themselves from voter rolls, do your crosschecking electronically. For example, to microtarget Italian Americans, look for Italian surnames in the voter file, add names of Italian organization members, and put in publicly commercial data such as lists of people who subscribe to Italian newspapers or magazines. That leaves more time for handwritten postcards. Same outreach, new technology, and always most effective with a personal touch.

Keep in mind that microtargeting only works with input from people on the ground, in the communities. A classic cautionary tale comes from Democratic strategist Donnie Fowler, who has worked in the field on every presidential campaign since 1988. Fowler recounted a story he heard when he first arrived in Iowa for the presidential caucuses: "A candidate preparing to broadcast a pro-choice message thought he had a receptive audience in an eastern Iowa community full of single women Democratic voters . . . until a closer look revealed that the precinct was a convent full of nuns."[18]

Although the nuns will know that your candidate is pro-choice—as would anyone reading your campaign Web site—targeting them with a pro-choice message will reflect badly on your campaign. The lesson, says Fowler, is that even if a high percentage of people agree with your position on an issue, your campaign is wasting resources by broadcasting the same message to 100 percent of them. You have to narrowcast, based on input from people on the ground. In the nuns' case, this input saved the candidate major embarrassment. Fowler concludes: "Campaigning is an art and a science—the science is the data, and the art is the local wisdom."[19]

GUT CHECK: CAN YOU LEAD A CAMPAIGN TO VICTORY?

Now that you have inventoried and toured your community, do you have a visceral understanding of the people in your community? Take a hard look at the data and ask yourself, can my cause or candidate succeed?

Now match your visceral understanding with political reality. Do you have the relationships necessary to take the top leadership role in campaigning for a ballot measure or as a candidate for office? Do you have the optimal relationships, experience, and track record in your community to put together the message, management, money, and mobilization that are needed to win?

If you are making a decision as a candidate, be clear about your aptitudes. California progressive strategist Alex Clemens, who founded the Usual Suspects Web site tracking San Francisco Bay Area politics and policy, offers the following advice to aspiring leaders: "Identify the issues you would take to the barricades. Determine if you are the best person to take the lead for your issue on this campaign: go to your mountaintop, speak to your rabbis [mentors], and be honest with yourself. If this is a fit, go for it. If not, find the person who is the best fit, and support them."[20]

In that vein, former New York congressman Dan Maffei told me that when he decided to run, he was told by a key mentor: "Assume that you are on your own." That's a lesson for all campaigns: even with all the networks and party registration numbers that portend success, in the end you have to take personal responsibility to earn every vote and raise each dollar on your own.

If you are consulted by prospective candidates, don't be a dream killer. This decision is too personal for anyone to make for another. Lay out the risks, be sure they have thought through their options and let them decide how to pursue their dreams. Otherwise, they will think it is you—not their own lack of readiness—that prevented them from going down that path; and in addition to harming your relationship, you will hinder their ability to grow. I never tell candidates not to run—but I do ask them for strategies needed to achieve a win number and to recruit the people needed to talk to strangers, walk in the rain, and sleep on floors. If the numbers add up, it is time to recruit people from their community to the cause and empower them with leadership roles in the campaign. If now is not the time, they may wish to gain public service experience by working with a cause or candidate who shares their visions, ideas, and values.

★ ★ ★

GET REAL:
MAP YOUR POLITICAL GEOGRAPHY

Step 1 is to use this checklist to prepare a Community Inventory.

The People

★ How many people live in your community?

★ How old are they? How many are seniors? Families? Kids?

★ What is the ethnic breakdown of the district?

★ How many are renters and how many homeowners?

★ What is the per capita income?

★ What are the major schools?

★ Who are the 10 largest employers in the private, public, and nonprofit sectors?

★ What are 5 fastest growing small business opportunities?

★ What are the local unions and their membership figures? Which unions work what jobs?

★ What are active military, civil defense, and veteran populations?

★ Who are first responders?

The Geography

★ Is the community urban, suburban, rural, or a combination?

★ What are the parkland, beaches, and other recreation areas?

★ What are the transit routes?

★ What are the political districts (Supervisor/Assembly/ Congress/etc.)?

★ What are the population and growth centers?

★ What infrastructure is critical or integral to national security?

★ What are the historical museums, landmarks, and tourist attractions?

The Traditions

★ What are the community traditions: the Big Game, annual neighborhood or ethnic festivals, Fourth of July parades, chamber picnics, beach cleanups, 5K races?

★ What are the cultural landmarks, places of worship, and institutions: universities, think tanks, foundations, civic engagement organizations, and business associations?

The Opinion Leaders

★ Who are the opinion leaders: newspaper columnists, philanthropists, labor leaders, corporate leaders, nonprofit directors, civil rights and human rights leaders?

★ Who leads the community institutions that participate in these traditions (block club presidents, church deacons, shop stewards, PTA presidents)?

★ Which online networks have vibrant followings in your community?

★ What are the campus networks?

The Politics

★ How many voters are eligible, registered, and voting?

★ How have similar candidates and initiatives performed in the past?

★ Are voters likely to support you or your opposition in an upcoming election?

★ What election technology is used?

★ How do people vote: early, absentee, by mail?

★ Are there any restrictions or expansions to voting rights since the last election?

★ Are there changes in polling places or time of operation?

★ Is there a deciding voting bloc that can determine the outcome of the election?

★ Who are the people elected at the local, county, state, and federal levels?

★ What are the various political camps in your community, and who is on which side?

★ Will you be forced to choose sides, and which side shares your values?

★ Which of these political leaders are likely to get involved in your campaign?

★ What is your win number: how many votes do you, your candidate, or your cause need to succeed?

Step 2 is to connect with community service leaders.

★ Do you know the community leaders you identified?

★ What challenges are most on their minds?

★ What work on issues have you done in the community?

★ What fund-raising or organizational work have you done for these community groups and leaders?

★ What work have you done with the online communities in your area?

★ What work have you done for (or against) these political leaders?

Finally, step 3 is a gut check: do you have a visceral understanding of your people?

★ How well do you know the people and traditions in your Community Inventory?

★ How familiar are you with the ideals and ideas of the people?

★ Are you the best person to step forward for your cause or candidate?

★ *Can you win?*

FOUR

★ ★ ★

Build Your Leadership Teams

Innovation distinguishes between
a leader and a follower.

STEVE JOBS

To win you must lead—and to lead you must innovate. A confident leader draws upon the best resources available and welcomes the guidance of innovative experts whose associating, questioning, observing, networking, and experimenting will propel the campaign forward. As a practical matter this means you recruit a diverse team of people who have demonstrated success in their profession and leadership in their community and you make sure the egos blend well in the cauldron of crisis. Candidates who think they know it all and surround themselves with people who reinforce that self-deception are doomed to fail.

Ultimately, the candidate or the campaign leader must weigh all advice and make the decision. GreenDog Campaigns' Dotty LeMieux reminds us: "The old adage 'Too many cooks spoil the broth' is true in politics as in cooking. Of course you want to get input from others, but some candidates just can't seem to say 'no.' They forget there's a chain of command, and want to take everyone's advice. They're nervous and insecure and it shows."[1]

A cause or campaign requires managers who have both functional expertise to do the job and real-world experience to anticipate problems and to come up with solutions.

The campaign manager cannot be the candidate and should not be anyone whom the candidate cannot fire. Family members, business partners, and best friends are invaluable helpers in the kitchen cabinet and on the trail, and should be compensated for advancing expenses or pitching in between staffers; but unless you can fire them, it is better not to hire them (and in some jurisdictions the law may set limits). Most start-up campaigns begin with the candidate or principal doing just about everything but quickly morph into a constellation of actors both paid and unpaid. The minute you have money, hire a campaign manager who can draft a winning plan. With that plan, hire fund-raisers early on, and use the funds for stipends to volunteers. Bring on campaign consultants later as funds allow.

Most people will not be compensated in the early weeks of a campaign. Political contributions of money and time are *not tax deductible* so you will be starting out with a core of true believers.

CONFIDENT LEADERS PICK COMPETENT PEOPLE

Your teams reflect your ability to recognize innovative leadership talent and to recruit and retain the best people to your cause, and in a broader sense, the most credible ambassadors for the larger social movement of public service. Carefully recruit people to your campaign staff and volunteer corps who share your values and ethics. No matter what job or volunteer function they have, the people you attract are your ambassadors. Look at their work histories, speak with their references, and ask them questions that matter to you.

Remember, you are responsible for whatever your team does that affects the outcome of your campaign and the ultimate realization of your vision. Your team members must demonstrate consistently good judgment; otherwise, you could find yourself defending against criticisms of your own managerial judgment caused by the reckless statements or the untrustworthy behavior of your own team. How can you tell whether a prospect has good judgment? Sometimes you just have to ask (within the law of course).

When it comes to vetting talent, retired state senator Art Torres, who served as longtime chair of the California Democratic Party and is currently a cochair of the stem cell research entity California Institute for Regenerative Medicine, asks people the most basic questions: "Who are you? What do you believe in? Is there anything I could read in the papers about you I'm not going to like?" This straightforward approach sparks conversations with candidates and staff that have less to do with past mistakes—we all make them—but much more to do with lessons learned.

For guidance, many jobs will have questionnaires and personnel manuals. If you are running for federal office, consider using the Office of Personnel Management Public Trust Positions questionnaire discussion in chapter 2. Otherwise, consult with people who hire managers at established nonprofits. Ask to see their personnel manuals and use them as models for interviews. Remember to ask an employment attorney first so you are not asking questions that run afoul of the law. Your local or state bar association has an employment law section that may have a pro bono help line or consultation. Use it.

More likely you will be vetting people by what you see them do online. Some people are shocked to find that their prospective employers Google them before an interview, but what they say online or under a pseudonym is public information. It is out there and fair game.

The bottom line is that you need to attract good people and to be as straightforward with them as you ask them to be with you. Campaigns are stressful enough on the best days—the best building blocks of leadership teams are trust, candor, and compassion.

CAMPAIGN STAFF
AND VOLUNTEER LEADERSHIP TEAM

Each of the campaign metrics—management, message, money, and mobilization—requires leadership teams. Management requires a *campaign staff* and *volunteer leadership team* to form a winning plan as well as a *kitchen cabinet* of trusted advisers to assist with sensitive decisions. Message requires *house meeting hosts* to bring the campaign into the community. Money requires a *finance council* to raise the funds necessary for success. Mobilization requires a vibrant *volunteer corps.* For a ballot initiative or candidate, mobilization also requires an *election protection team* to be sure that supporters vote and that their votes are counted as cast.

Each team must organize people around a shared vision, work with them in a disciplined way, build a culture of service within the campaign, and help achieve the vision.

Columnist George F. Will summarizes candidate leadership qualities as the physical stamina and the abilities to think strategically, to be tactically nimble, to select good staff members, to use their advice and criticism, and to respond to surprises and setbacks.[2] Your job is to recruit a campaign staff and a volunteer leadership team to hardwire leadership attributes—physical stamina, strategic thinking, nimble tactics, good recruitment, and responsiveness to surprises and setbacks—into a winning plan.

Physical stamina. A winning campaign will require an aggressive schedule to advance your message. The principal should be the hardest worker on the team. As AFSCME political director Larry Scanlon often reminds campaign leaders: "Don't ask people to do anything that you are not willing to do yourself."

You and your team members need the physical stamina for this marathon of a campaign. You will be working sixteen-hour days for months at a time. Be sure that you have the commitment to service and family support for this. With limited exceptions—brief workouts, weekly worship, family celebrations, and holidays—you will have to give over your personal time to the campaign.

"I should see you out and about in the community more than I see my own family," declares former California Assembly Speaker and San Francisco Mayor Willie L. Brown, Jr. Brown heard the call to serve during the civil rights struggle of the 1950s and was in elected office for thirty years while winning over a dozen elections himself and fielding a team of eighty legislative candidates every two years during his fifteen years as Speaker. "The more people who can see you are working for them, the better."[3]

In addition to physical stamina, you and your team will need emotional maturity. While there is a natural bonding that goes on during campaigns, many candidates or advisers have been known to stray from mentoring into romance. Though circumstances vary, as a general rule it is always more trouble than it's worth. You could violate workplace harassment laws and betray your loved ones and supporters. There are no secrets on campaigns—in earlier eras they may have been kept to a close circle, but that is no longer the case: the truth has a way of coming out. Best to devote your energies to the larger cause, and to remember that anyone is expendable, even you.

If you are working on a cause, you may not have a timetable as concrete as a specific Election Day. That gives you all the more reason to demonstrate stamina as you move through the political process, creating coalitions one person at a time to bring about social change.

Strategic thinking. The primary purpose of a campaign staff and volunteer leadership team is to craft a campaign plan that lays out a strategy to win. Former San Francisco Supervisor Jim Gonzalez advises, "A campaign plan must answer who, what, when, where, why, and how you are going to put forward the best message and deliver that message as many times as possible to as many of your identified supporters as possible."[4]

Be nimble. In the words of AFSCME's Larry Scanlon, you must be "nimble, creative, and opportunistic" because you can't take the politics out of politics.[5] No matter how well thought-out your plan, political considerations will require you to shift gears.

★ ★ ★ ★ ★ ★ ★ ★ ★ ★ ★ ★

CAMPAIGN JOBS, JOB DESCRIPTIONS, AND CRITICAL SKILLS

To start you may have paid staff consisting of your Campaign Manager, Scheduler, Operations Director, Field Director, Campaign Counsel, Finance Director, Research [aka Policy] Director, Database Manager, Communications Director, Online Operations Director, Treasurer, and Volunteer Coordinator:

Campaign Manager. NOT the candidate or anyone the candidate cannot fire. Drafts and implements the campaign plan. Runs day-to-day operations. Oversees recruitment and retention of all staff and key volunteer leaders, mentoring, and coaching of talent. Engages team around shared values, builds interdependent teams, creates dynamic strategies, and mobilizes people through meaningful action. Keeps campaign on track toward its goals and ensures efficient decision making and action taking. Needs a thick skin and an open-door policy. (See chapters 2–7.)

Scheduler. Manages campaign calendar. Creates opportunities to advance message via candidate and surrogates. Assists candidate or manager with phone and written queries from community, i.e., prospective voters, endorsers, and donors. Has event planning experience and diplomatic people skills. (See chapters 2 and 4.)

Operations Director. Responsible for administration of physical place used for headquarters and the procurement and maintenance of computers and communications equipment, security of IT and personnel, storage, and utilities. Manages payroll. (See chapter 4.)

Field Director. Mobilizes volunteers to bring out voters, organizes house meetings, and manages get-out-the-vote efforts. (See chapters 4 and 7.)

Campaign Counsel. Handles filing of all legal documents required to run for office or to file ballot initiative and coordinates "Election Protection" team. Should have technical expertise in elections law. (See chapters 6 and 7.)

▶

▸ **Finance Director.** Works with finance council to identify and secure new sources of funding, follows up on pledged contributions, and leverages technology to simplify the process of giving money to the campaign. Has experience managing resources and leveraging donations. (See chapters 4 and 5.)

Research [aka Policy] Director. Directs research on people and issues to fuel policy development and message development, such as creation, maintenance, and deployment of voter and donor database, monitoring of competitive messaging, positions, and policy issues, interaction with policy experts, and briefing leadership team, organizes surrogates for messaging opportunities. (See chapters 2, 3, and 4.)

Database Manager. Maintains political data, voter records, contributor records, volunteer lists, and fund-raising lists. (See chapters 4, 6, and 7.)

Communications Director. Directs paid and free media operations. Facilitates direct communication with press, volunteers, and networks. Works on message refinement, public relations, event planning and scheduling, speech writing, Web site maintenance, media planning and production, development of promotional kits and "chum," cited tchotchkes on the East Coast, swag on the West Coast. (See chapters 2, 6, and 7.)

Online Operations Director. Manages Web site, directs online organizing and digital campaign strategies, develops a theory of change, communications and new media outreach, engages e-mail list, social media strategies, and integration with on-the-ground field efforts. (See chapters 2–7.)

Treasurer. Keeps accounting records, does bookkeeping, issues checks, and files campaign financial disclosures. (See chapter 6.)

Volunteer Coordinator. Recruits, schedules, and supervises volunteers. Builds leadership teams of volunteers. Recognizes volunteers for their service. Patient teacher and enthusiastic supporter. (See chapters 4 and 7.)

★ ★ ★ ★ ★ ★ ★ ★ ★ ★ ★

DEVELOPING A CAMPAIGN PLAN

Let's say that your campaign plan is for a ballot initiative. Your potential supporters are people in your political party and people in communities and constituencies who have historically voted your way in the past, and your plan must deliver them to the polls and deliver their vote to your cause and not to your competitor's. These are the questions that your management team must answer to plan for success:

★ *Who?* Of those people eligible to vote, determine who might vote for you or your cause. Start with the microtargeting work you did to crosscheck your voter file with your Community Inventory data, publicly available consumer information, personal Rolodexes, membership lists, and input from individual volunteers who have reached these voters directly. Identify people who will never vote for someone from your party, who will never support your position on the ballot issue, who never make it to the polls, or who are not legally allowed to vote. They are not your targets. When it comes to swing voters, you will have to discuss values and issues that may move them. Who will you target?

★ *What?* Your campaign must develop a message that enables you to win. What will your message be?   ▶

Shifting gears means a big donor pulls her funding, so you find the money someplace else; a newspaper editorial slams your ballot initiative, so you increase media buys to counter the effect; someone jumps into your race, so you keep your supporters on your team; someone drops out, so you chase their supporters. Your plan should be flexible enough to turn fast when needed. As President Bill Clinton often cautioned Democrats, "Assume that the other side is working just as hard as you are" to think fast, react forcefully, and seize opportunities.[6]

▶ ★ **Where?** You must reach your targeted supporters where they live and where they get their political information, whether that means knocking on their doors, appearing on their television sets, visiting them online, or texting their cell phones. Your Media Plan will lay out who gets their information from what sources. Where will your campaign contact people?

★ **When?** You should deliver your message to your targeted supporters as many times as possible. Consult the Community Inventory traditions and your campaign calendar for events where you need to be. When will you start your communications program?

★ **Why?** Winning is the reason for everything you do in a campaign for a ballot initiative or candidate. If some activity does not clearly contribute to victory or, after a certain point, starts to erode its own contribution, then stop doing it and test a new approach. For example, if people complain about your nasty ads, you may have to go positive. Or if they complain about robo-calls, you need live phone banks instead.

★ **How?** What is the "win number" (one vote over 50 percent, a plurality, etc.) to carry your cause or candidate to victory? How, given limited resources, will you achieve it?

Bottom line: Can you reach your win number on Election Day?

Recruit well. Choose good people who can work together as a team for long hours under intense pressure. Test the chemistry of the team so that people with shared ethics and values also have good teamwork. Many a campaign hired great talents whose egos got in the way of the cause, leaving the shuddering staffers waiting for "mom and dad to stop fighting in front of us," as one young man described it.

Everyone will be an advocate for a particular part of the campaign: message people will want polls and media ads; mobilization people will want field program dollars. Choose people who can debate tactics without scaring the campaign "kids," and then leave internal discussions behind to emerge as "one team, one fight."

As national communications strategist Jamal Simmons advises, "People will tell you the truth—either to your face or behind your back. It's up to you to create an environment where they can tell you to your face." For instance, when Simmons worked for Mickey Kantor, commerce secretary in the Clinton-Gore administration, he was told "don't blow smoke" by his boss, who wanted an honest critique of his performance after speeches and interviews.[7]

Respond positively to surprises and setbacks. Every public service effort has its bad days. One of those unwelcome surprises turns up in the news one day, and the campaign morale plummets. It may not even be a crisis but a disappointment: you work your heart out for an endorsement, and it goes to the other side. You raise less money than you thought; you get a bad poll; your allies have other priorities. If you believe in what you are doing, you will have the strength to fall and get back up numerous times. Successful campaigns respond to surprises and setbacks by remaining optimistic and true to their service mission, and by addressing problems up front.

You need your team to face surprises and setbacks directly, and that means you must face them directly. Likewise, if you have bad news, take it directly to the leadership team. "Don't spin the bad news," cautions Lezlee Westine. Reflecting on her experience as a senior adviser to President George W. Bush, Westine recommends giving the news "first, fast, straightforward, simple, and solution-oriented."[8] First—because getting bad news from allies beats getting blindsided by enemies. Fast, straightforward, and simple—because people need to understand what they are up against. Solution-oriented—because people are relying on you to help them figure out how to address the problem. They expect you to exercise candor and judgment, so be up front about what's wrong and what can be done to make it right. If you have a more serious crisis brewing, it's time to bring in the kitchen cabinet.

KITCHEN CABINET

A *kitchen cabinet* is a management team of trusted friends, colleagues, and family members who know how you receive advice and criticism and can speak truth to power when necessary. They know your character—your core values and vision, your code of ethics, and your sensitivity to feedback, be it positive, negative, or unsolicited. They are the people to whom you already turn when you need advice, constructive criticism, or guidance in difficult situations. They volunteer their advice on critical issues with a minimum of gossip and a maximum of discretion, assist with rapid response to surprises, and otherwise help to avert or to manage crises.

In assembling your kitchen cabinet, ask yourself:

★ How do I receive advice and criticism?

★ Who are the people I already engage in that process?

★ Whom do I trust to give me constructive criticism?

★ If I make a mistake, whose advice should I take?

★ When I get stuck, who gets me unstuck?

★ When I am in crisis, who convinces me to stop doing what I am doing, put my future ahead of my anger, and take a long view to my life dreams?

Then, break down your answers in the following categories:

Your friends. In public life, there are "first-name friends" and "last-name friends." *First-name friends* are those who know and appreciate you for you: they know you outside politics, and their personal ambition does not depend on your professional success. *Last-name friends* know and appreciate you for your public persona or service agenda and can

be great allies, but they may not necessarily be trusted
advisers. Every prospective candidate or campaign leader
needs both first-name friends and last-name friends, but add
only first-name friends to your kitchen cabinet.

Your family. Which family members give you good personal
and professional advice? While you will solicit (and receive
unsolicited) advice from many family members, you may
not want them all in the same room with each other or with
your campaign team. Be open to hearing all their concerns
but pick a couple for your kitchen cabinet. Again, think of
these as concentric circles: you want the chemistry to work
and can't have too many cooks. Sometimes only a family
member can call you out for failing to maintain work-life
balance or tell you that your decision making is off because
you haven't slept in three days.

Your mentors. Which of your political or civic mentors have
managed public service campaigns and dealt with political
crises? Include a couple of them in your kitchen cabinet
and be in touch with as many as you can. They know how
you make decisions and sometimes can be good sounding
boards for ideas because they are not in your fray every
day. They are the people who remind you how you failed
and recovered in the past, or keep your wits and humor
intact with advice like that of the late Israeli prime minister
Golda Meir, who said, "Don't act so humble, you're not that
great." Mentors who know the rhythms of the particular
campaign you are working can be helpful guides. Others
may just provide sympathetic ears. But all are important to
keep you on track.

Your allies. Sometimes our philosophical opponents see us
more clearly than we see ourselves. Allies from the opposite
side of the aisle can provide a reality check on your policies
because their success does not depend on the outcome of
your campaign.

Those who know don't talk, and those who talk don't know. The ideal is a kitchen cabinet whose members provide unvarnished feedback and bad news along with constructive solutions with a minimum of gossip and a maximum of discretion. As with any other internal deliberation, advice should be offered behind the scenes, not in the newspapers. Advice should be discreet and direct—a discreet conversation with a direct approach to the issues at hand.

The old adage about Watergate—"The cover-up was worse than the crime"—is a sharp reminder to today's crisis managers. If you face a crisis, get out in front of it: set forth your version of events, provide supporting documentation if applicable, communicate with your supporters and the public, and get back on track.

Rapid response is vital in our twenty-four-hour image cycle. The arc of a scandal is generally the same: recognition, responsibility, recommitment, and redemption. There must be recognition of the issue with candor and contrition as appropriate, responsibility for any mistakes, recommitment to service, and redemption. People tend to want to move on and focus on their future, and they will more likely do so if they can trust their public servants to do so as well. Any delay—or relapse—in this narrative will be politically dangerous.

HOUSE MEETING HOSTS

Your strategy must bring your message into the community, introduce you to your neighbors, and attract volunteers to your campaign. There is no more intimate setting than the homes of your constituents and no better stage than their living rooms and backyards for practicing your pitch, testing new ideas, and refining your message to your community.

House meeting hosts can become full partners in your campaign—and in your career. In 1987, farmworkers union organizer Fred Ross Jr. ran a grassroots house meeting operation for the Nancy Pelosi for Congress special election campaign. Over

★ ★ ★ ★ ★ ★ ★ ★ ★ ★ ★ ★ ★

COMPONENTS OF A SUCCESSFUL
HOUSE MEETING STRATEGY

Your strategy includes these components: Community Outreach, Coordinators, Hosts, Message, Goals, Script, Materials, Scheduling, Feedback, and Follow-up.

Community Outreach. Grassroots outreach begins at home. Public service is often a family call to service: it is not unusual to have several generations participating. Opening one's home is an act of community and trust. Guests and campaign representatives should be mindful of the confidence placed in you by your hosts and sponsors.

Coordinators. Your team's house meeting coordinators will recruit hosts, put together house meeting packets, map out where meetings are held, keep track of how many volunteers are recruited, report guests' feedback, and handle campaign follow-up. A handful of well-trained volunteers can perform this function as a team, with responsibility divided along geographic or political lines across the community.

Hosts. Start with your networks: your family, friends, work colleagues, and nonprofit allies. Build off your Community Inventory and leadership teams. House meeting hosts are your ambassadors, so think family, friends, neighbors, political club or network colleagues, union members, mavens who tend to host meet-ups, students, seniors, and veterans, as well as people you supported in past service efforts.

Some people don't feel comfortable having people they don't know come into their home but are happy to host a meeting at a community center, a local coffee house, union hall, community room in a housing complex, or a campus deli.

Message. Make your pitch. First, express your call to service. Then explain your campaign plan to win. Third, engage the audience on values and issues. ▶

▸ **Goals.** Win elections (Pelosi, Obama), organize causes (MLK, UFW), and grow membership (nonprofits, clubs). In a campaign that needs a thousand volunteers, you will need to schedule 100 house meetings, and recruit an average of ten people from each one. Successful hosts can lead regional headquarters offices and/ or become house-meeting coordinators. If it's an underdog campaign, get everyone to put up signs all at once as a show of force.

Script. This is no freestyle coffee klatch or gab session; it is your job interview. Have fun and follow this template: (1) The host welcomes all. (2) People tell why they are present. (3) The campaign rep makes the house meeting pitch and plays a campaign DVD. (4) The host facilitates a Q&A. (5) The campaign rep gives thanks and a final "ask" for support. (6) A new host volunteers.

Materials. You'll need invitations—the more personal the better; a candidate biography, nonprofit firm résumé, or ballot measure summary; DVD of ads and/or testimonials; literature, bumper stickers, buttons, lapel stickers, signs, and chum/tchotckes/swag; notable news articles; volunteer cards and remittance envelopes.

Scheduling. The scheduler, coordinators, and hosts together should make a campaign master schedule of all house meetings. Remember, your goal is to win, so schedule house meetings to advance your message and recruit volunteers to turn out the votes you need. Place the schedule online so people can find/create events. Try holding a big night of multiple meetings with a live phone-in conference call featuring an all-star.

Feedback. A well-intentioned kick can make your message better and your campaign stronger. The host and coordinator should review turnout (Did we get people there and recruit them? Who wasn't there who we should be including?), program (Did people understand our message?), and systems (Did we make new recruits feel welcome?).

Follow-up. Be sure to send out thank-you notes. Keep an open feedback loop, and make sure all the questions get answered via e-mail or phone. Tell house meeting hosts that you performed the follow-up they requested. Their guests will hold them accountable for your response!

120 house meetings were held in six weeks. Nearly twenty-five years later, dozens of those hosts are still engaged in her ongoing community events. You might think house meetings are old school—and you'd be right—but they still work better than anything else I've seen to connect and inspire people.

For example, at a South Carolina Democratic Party–sponsored boot camp on primary eve in January 2008, strategist Donnie Fowler and I presented to volunteers and observers, including supporters of Hillary Clinton, Barack Obama, and John Edwards. When I talked about finding strangers to give house meetings, a Clinton volunteer said, "We don't do those here." "We did," said an Obama supporter.

Since Clinton and Edwards had nearly all the opinion leaders who could turn out their people via top-down operations, the Obama campaign had to organize bottom-up with house meetings in order to change the tide of the election.

Three days later, I was discussing Obama's decisive South Carolina victory win at a reception with Martin Luther King III and United Farm Workers of America's Arturo Rodriguez. "Obama won using the house meetings we did twenty years ago for my mom's campaign with UFW support," I said. "[UFW founder] César [Chavez] did them forty years ago to start the farm workers," Rodriguez chimed in. "And my parents did them fifty years ago during the civil rights marches," added Martin King. What was "innovative" to some in 2008 was actually a reincarnation of a bottom-up grassroots strategy that worked in 1987, 1968, 1956, and probably before that. So before you reject house meetings as "old school" consider the rich history and successful results, then innovate adapting to new times.

Technology makes for more interconnected house meetings. For example, in 2010 the Barbara Boxer for Senate campaign combined old-school organizing with new media tools. She held concurrent house meetings around the state where supporters watched her campaign videos, heard from guest speakers, and then got a conference call linking the house meetings together featuring the candidate herself to maximize impact.

House meetings also work for issue campaigns because the intimacy makes them excellent organizing tools for screening films that promote social change, such as former vice president Al Gore's Academy Award–winning documentary, *An Inconvenient Truth*.

Plan your campaign's strategy for recruiting house meeting hosts. First, take a look at your kitchen cabinet and other leadership teams. Each person who lives in your community should be asked to host or help host a house meeting that can serve as a recruiting vehicle for small donors and volunteers. Second, take a look at your Community Inventory. Whom did you identify as the Opinion Leaders? Who are the people who know people? Who is the person who always hosts house meetings? Whose efforts have you helped who might return the favor? Third, conduct meetings and recruit house meeting hosts from there. You should always end a meeting with a commitment to hold another one.

While some campaigns consider house meetings to be closed to press, everyone is a citizen journalist these days. Assume the proceedings are recorded and on the record. Also, have the host facilitate questions because oftentimes people will show far more politeness to a host extending them hospitality than they will to a candidate. While most people are civil, there are a few who take it upon themselves to vent. Hosts should be ready to move the conversation along.

Be sure that people leave with a creative memento of the campaign. Bumper stickers are great—if they actually go on cars. Stickers are more common than lapel pins in a low-budget campaign. Other ideas include hats, T-shirts, potholders, and unisex nail files—all made in America with union labor.

Reach voters in their native language. If you do not speak it, then recruit a respected leader from the community to translate on your behalf. At a house meeting in a bilingual neighborhood,

★ ★ ★ ★ ★ ★ ★ ★ ★ ★ ★ ★

CREATIVE OUTREACH

The hand: In Idaho, Larry LaRocco was running for lieutenant governor. He had a card with a hand on it that read "25,000 hands/25,000 Idaho stories" that he gave to everyone. Each hand—representing a handshake—was numbered, so people felt engaged when they got #324 or #67. They would greet him by shouting, "I'm #324!" "Remember me? I'm #67." Months after the campaign, people still identified themselves by the personalized number.*

The fan: In the South, many candidates distribute "funeral fans"—named because they would be passed out at sweltering services. Originally the fans had the name of the funeral home on them; now they have candidate names and causes.

The pint: Some candidates distribute pints of liquor with their campaign information plastered on them—a colorful tradition now adapted to a nonalcoholic version. For example, at a 2006 win-the-House event, Congresswoman Barbara Lee served up miniature champagne bottles filled with sparkling cider labeled with Speaker-to-be Nancy Pelosi's face superimposed on a Rosie the Riveter image on the label.

The song: Although each candidate will have his or her "walk on music" for large events and rallies, nothing beats a homegrown campaign song. For instance, Hank Johnson, former DeKalb County, Georgia, commissioner and now a congressman, had a song encapsulating his message titled "Taking Care of Home." A downloadable MP3 recording of the song was on Hank Johnson's Web site.[†]

The map: One way to show you're taking care of home is a map of your community with landmarks indentifying the work you've done. Congressman George Miller used a simple map of his Northern California district to show the places where he'd worked to improve schools, repair bridges, fund community centers, and so forth. ▶

▶ Nowadays you can update Miller's innovation using Google Earth mapping to provide a digital report to demonstrate the impact of your service in people's lives.

The video: In 1988, Anna Eshoo ran for Congress in the Silicon Valley. She put together a video, "Anna Eshoo Will Challenge the Sacred Cows." The video was the first of its kind. A pollster asked whether people had video machines, and volunteers delivered 110,000 VHS cassettes in just two weekends. The campaign generated media buzz and voter excitement. "People thought: 'If she can think that way in how she communicates with us, imagine what she'll do when she represents us,'" remembers Eshoo, who now serves as a top Democrat on the Communications and Technology Subcommittee in Congress.[‡]

The personalized poster: The 2004 Bush-Cheney campaign had an interactive computer program called the Sloganator on their Web site that invited supporters to personalize their posters. People could go online and create their own personal poster for the campaign. Although the tricksters got to it, creating posters not in keeping with the campaign's messages, the two-way outreach was a great innovation.[§]

The nail file: In California, Rosalind Wyman ran for city council in the 1960s. She passed out nail files imprinted with her name. Years later, in races for Democratic National Committee, Wyman reprised the nail files and slogans. Although the 1996 slogan, "Let's nail down Clinton's reelection," was apt for its time, many an activist made use of the file emblazoned with "With Roz Wyman on the DNC, this election won't be a nail biter" during the recounts of 2000.

*Larry LaRocco, e-mail, July 23, 2007.

[†]Hank Johnson for Congress Web site. www.hankforcongress.com/multimedia/campaignsong.

[‡]Anna Eshoo, interview, July 22, 2007.

[§]Daniel Kurtzman, "The Bush-Cheney Sloganator," *About.com*: Political Humor, March 15, 2004. http://politicalhumor.about.com/b/a/088547.htm.

bring bilingual materials, play your Spanish-language ads, or seek bilingual phone bankers to help build support.

Avoid offending blocs of voters by recruiting them from the start, hiring staff from diverse constituencies, and preparing materials with specific translations.

FINANCE COUNCIL

A public service campaign *finance council* is the team that raises the funds necessary for success. It creates and oversees the campaign budget and implements the campaign finance plan.

The financial council consists of a finance chair, a treasurer, a finance director, and key donors. The finance chair is a well-respected member of the community who has a track record in support of your public service mission. This person leads the fund-raising effort. The treasurer balances the books, issues checks, and files campaign disclosure reports. The finance director works with the finance council to identify new sources of potential contributions and to bring that money into the campaign. Start with your informal finance council people with whom you have raised funds for other causes and candidates.

The goal of a good campaign is to spend exactly what is needed—and not a penny more—to win. As with the campaign plan, your budget should express a clear strategy to capture the votes needed to win the election or to complete your concrete service mission. (Represent X number of indigent clients, do X number of trainings, place X number of books in public schools, maintain X number of organic gardens, etc.) It should cover the staff and materials required by each of the four major parts of your campaign: message, management, money, and mobilization.

In considering recruits for your finance council consider these questions:

★ Who are the people who sit on finance councils for campaigns like mine?

★ Who among my kitchen cabinet is a good fund-raiser or can
   recommend one?

★ Who in my Community Inventory is known for donating to
   causes I believe in?

★ Who is able to leverage "in kind" (not cash) contributions of
   food or services?

★ Who has an active network and can send e-mails on my
   behalf?

★ Are there networks (see chapter 5) that invite candidates or
   campaign reps for meet-and-greets? One of their leaders
   would be helpful.

★ Who can advise on the proper mix of network TV (old
   media) buys and new media buys, especially if I pay my
   media consultant on commission?

Potential supporters looking at campaigns want to see how
much money goes for old media versus new media in the communications budget. One old school campaign strategy I can
do without is the overreliance on heavy old media buys with
management commissions. I once invited a candidate to a boot
camp, and his field director accepted. Three days later the campaign manager called saying the field director was gone and he
wasn't sure the candidate needed my boot camp: "He is going to
spend $3 million on this race. When that goes to media I get 15
percent commission. What will he learn at your boot camp that
will help my campaign plan?" Well, geez, when you put it that
way. . . . I gave Mr. 15 percent credit for being honest. He saw
no need to invest in field operations and didn't want to lose "his"
campaign plan, aka his commission. While few will be as blunt,
many think like Mr. 15 percent.

As craigslist founder Craig Newmark comments, "I hope that buzz and social media will be more important and less expensive than television. Campaign consultants still make too much money on TV buys, and they will in 2012, but I am hoping that in 2016 we will see candidates directing buys primarily to social media." If given the choice between a candidate spending a million dollars on TV versus a candidate spending a million dollars on new media, Newmark "would go with the new media candidate because moving our politics online makes it cheaper and more exposed to truth telling."[9]

The following percentages are meant to provide you with a rough guideline to creating a strong budget: management: 10 percent; message/media: 60 percent; money: 10 percent; mobilization: 20 percent. To stretch that 60 percent, you can use cable instead of network television and use new media buys: banner ads on microtargeted Web sites and social networks like iPhone apps, YouTube videos, Twitter hashtags, Facebook and text messaging to rev up support.

Republican Senator Scott Brown of Massachusets did this in 2010. He created the "Brown Brigade" where "Brown's staff could reach his supporters, his supporters could respond to him, and supporters could find one another to organize." They sent text messages to supporters when he or his opponent was on the radio with the show's number to call in and multiply his message.[10] That money was likely far better leveraged than if it had been spent on network television.

How you recruit your finance council sends a message about whether you want communication with your voters to be "one to many" (you send a message out to many people on TV or radio or e-mail) or "many to many" (your networks send messages to their networks, all of whom communicate with you and each other). Adding new media gurus will help guide media spending that reflects the more modern crowd-sourced beehive model in which people are communicating in concentric circles and giving constant feedback. It will also help you save money, because new media gurus can wire your campaign and provide discounted or in-kind (free) services.

Remember that your budget must accurately reflect the various intervals of a campaign. Do you qualify for matching funds at a certain point? Is there a large fund-raiser scheduled for June 30, the last day of the quarter and an important finance filing deadline? You will face such issues in creating a working campaign budget.

Once you have created your budget, the campaign manager's job is to stick to it. For this reason, many campaigns have a rule that only the campaign manager can authorize expenditures. Not even the candidate should be able to spend—or promise to spend—money without getting the campaign manager's approval first. The campaign manager, in turn, should not have a conflict of interest if he is getting a piece of the action.

If you work with a nonprofit, your finance council is your quality-control team. It may be a subset of your board of directors and include your auditing and accounting staff. Monitor your expenses and maintain exquisite records. TechNet's Lezlee Westine said that, as CEO of a $3 million nonprofit, she checked her budget every week. That kind of scrupulous vigilance plus technology tools can help keep track of your finances and keep faith with your investors and the public.

VOLUNTEER CORPS COORDINATORS

A vibrant volunteer corps is the heart and soul of a public service campaign. The volunteer corps is generally led by the volunteer coordinator and includes trusted volunteers who believe in the campaign and have invested time training new people as they come in to the effort. These team leaders must be patient and enthusiastic.

Devote resources to recruiting, training, and motivating volunteer coordinators who, in turn, will give each potential volunteer a brief welcome interview, lay out the plan, experiment with different activities to find a match, and be patient and thankful.

Begin with people from your Community Inventory, opinion leaders who volunteer on campaigns like yours and already have good connections within the community and a willingness to share their Rolodexes. I met former San Francisco Supervisor Leslie Katz on the campaign trail twenty-five years ago. Well before running for office herself, she walked in the Nancy Pelosi campaign headquarters with her Rolodex one day and called through it to bring in volunteers. Now a San Francisco Port Commissioner with national experience organizing for LGBT equality, Katz continues to expand and share her Rolodex in pursuit of her call to service. You need to find volunteer corps coordinators like Katz who "graduated" from house meeting host to take on greater responsibility.

As discussed in chapter 1, many of your networks do campaign training programs that can help your team learn the ropes: political parties and political networks have trainings for specific campaign roles. The campaign should organize a boot camp for volunteer corps coordinators to show new team members the ropes and set up basic data management systems so that as people enter the system their areas of interest and levels of participation (house meetings, lawn signs, donations, door knocking) are all on file. That way the team is ready for, say, a veterans-to-veterans or women-to-women phone-banking night: a click of the mouse should pull up all the people for a particular constituency.

Cloud computing systems through Google allow people to schedule events together online, then meet up off-line, and phone services like FreeConferenceCall.com allow participants to set up virtual phone banks and training calls. You can use these free programs to initiate regularly scheduled events like a monthly call with the candidate or the initiative pollsters and the volunteers working with the grassroots.

Most campaigns skills can be divided into the 3 Ps: people, paper, and physical. Volunteer coordinators are the "people people" who work the phones, doors, and house meetings; paper people track voters, volunteers, and current events; and physical people deliver signs, secure supplies, or prep the headquarters for various activities. This method of mobilizing builds a culture of service within the campaign, where each person's contribution—to any of the leadership teams or organizational needs—is a message multiplier.

Devising some kind of recognition makes everyone feel good. Write names on stars and hang them in the office. Have a photo wall or a creative thermometer to show that the team met its goals of walking X precincts or stuffing X mailers. The Volunteer corps coordinators make the headquarters a place where people want to return for a positive experience even during the negative times of a campaign.

ELECTION PROTECTION TEAM

Voting is a civic sacrament—the highest responsibility we have as Americans. You must promote and protect the vote for all your constituents, whether they vote for you or not. Your *election protection team* comprised of voting experts and lawyers develops the strategy to ensure that supporters vote and that their votes are counted as cast.

If you work on a political campaign, you must know how and where the votes are being cast and counted. Begin with your campaign counsel. Add people who understand the voting patterns of the community, including representatives of constituency groups who have voting rights expertise and who can add counsel and help with get-out-the-vote efforts across the electorate. Expand to institutes that track voting rights issues. Particular areas of concern are early voting, military ballots, and student voting.

Do not save your get-out-the-vote efforts for the last days before Election Day. You must begin at the inception of your campaign.

From voter registration to vote recount, you must have this team keeping an eye on your votes at all times. This is where your national networks are helpful because they already "know the territory." If you call an election hotline, you can find someone who knows the election law in your community.

Democratic National Committee vice chair and voting rights advocate Donna Brazile describes voting as "one of our most sacred and important rituals" and cautions that voting is "still threatened every election day by uninformed poll workers, technology, campaigns more interested in winning than an individual's right, and election laws that don't always make sense."[11]

Moreover, in the last few years there has been an aggressive effort to restrict voting. According to the nonpartisan Brennan Center for Justice at New York University, legislators around the country have been pushing bills that make sweeping changes to their election codes to limit the voting rights of students and movers, reduce early voting days, and restrict voter registration and "get-out-the-vote" mobilization efforts that all told could restrict voting rights of 5 million Americans in 2012.[12]

The DNC's Voting Rights Institute report on voter ID laws is revealing: 11 percent of Americans—approximately 23 million citizens of voting age—lack proper photo ID and, as a result, could be turned away from the polls on Election Day. Those without photo ID are disproportionately low-income, disabled, minority, young, and older voters.[13]

Your team should know your opponent's views on these voting laws. Is she an advocate for reform or for restrictions? What roles has she played?

Even if some voter restrictions end up passing, they may backfire as people remember which party wanted them to vote and which one didn't. Look to the West, where GOP-backed Latinos for Reform ran despicable ads urging Latino voters not to vote in 2010.[14] Galvanized by longtime civil rights activists like Dolores Huerta, who called it a "deceptive trap of no representation," and new media networks like Voto Latino, Latino

★ ★ ★ CALL TO SERVICE ★ ★ ★

DONNA BRAZILE

Democratic National Committee vice chair Donna Brazile, who has spent a lifetime in politics offering her expertise as an author, pundit, and presidential campaign manager for Al Gore in 2000, traces her interest in voting rights to her youth:

> As a child growing up in the Deep South during the civil rights revolution, I wanted to get involved and help create the change that I was witnessing every day. On the night Dr. Martin Luther King Jr. was assassinated, I made a personal vow to God to work for change and to help make a difference. Soon I found myself working alongside other civil rights workers to register people to vote and helping out during election season. I was riveted by the passion of those civil rights workers who were both courageous and determined to have a seat at the table where public policy decisions were being made. They were my inspiration. Their sacrifice and commitment to the ideals of freedom and equality gave me hope for the future and led me to dedicate my own life to helping to keep the dream of justice and equality for all—regardless of race, gender, class, disability, age, or sexual orientation. We are all God's children, and no one deserves to be treated as a second-class citizen.

Source: http://www.brennancenter.org/blog/archives/states_legislatures_work _to_restrict_voting_rights/. "Voting Law Changes in 2012" http://www.brennan center.org/content/resource/voting_law_changes_in_2012.

voters *did* vote, and a majority gave their votes—and thus the Senate Majority—to pro-immigrant Democrats Harry Reid in Nevada, Barbara Boxer in California, and Michael Bennet in Colorado. The lesson expressed by Voto Latino's Maria Teresa Kumar applies to all voters: "Voting, no matter your political party or which candidate you support, is the most important civic tool that American Latinos have to be heard and understood by decision makers nationwide."[15]

You must check to know the current state of the law. Your election protection chair should brief the team on the law in your community so that you can prepare your volunteers and plan your campaign accordingly. Your campaign's veterans and military families advisory council should have representation on the election protection team. Consult with national networks such as the Overseas Vote Foundation and Democrats Abroad for the latest on the Federal Absentee Ballot for Americans temporarily abroad.

Your team should consult with disability rights advocates to ensure access for your voters. Wade Henderson, president of the Leadership Conference on Civil and Human Rights, and Mark Perriello, president of the American Association of People with Disabilities, wrote "Voter I.D. Laws Hurt Our Democracy," an op-ed in the *Progressive* (July 18, 2011). It points out:

> There are more than 30 million Americans with disabilities of voting age, yet the Federal Election Commission (FEC) reports that there are more than 20,000 inaccessible polling places. Some are located in basements or buildings without ramps, and others only offer machines that are outdated and unworkable for a person who is blind, deaf, or physically impaired. Too many citizens with disabilities can only cast their vote curbside or are denied the right to a secret ballot when they have to speak their vote out loud for someone else to mark down.
>
> If impediments were removed and people with disabilities began voting in the same proportion as other Americans, fully 3.2 million more people would be casting ballots.[16]

After all the hard work of your leadership teams to develop and implement the campaign plan, you will want to make sure that your public service campaign ends in victory, with every supporter voting and every vote counted as cast.

★ ★ ★

GET REAL:
BUILD YOUR LEADERSHIP TEAMS

Campaigns are often shaped by character and events. Campaign teams made up of people who know your character can best help you create and respond to events in a manner that will effectively promote your message.

1. Build Your Kitchen Cabinet

You need people you can trust to give unvarnished feedback and bad news along with constructive solutions with a minimum of gossip and a maximum of discretion. Consider:

★ People already in your informal kitchen cabinet
★ Key family members
★ Political or civic mentors
★ First-name friends who appreciate you outside of public life
★ An ally from the opposite side of the aisle who can provide a reality check

Who needs to be added to your kitchen cabinet, and what is your strategy to recruit them?

2. Recruit Your House Meeting Hosts

House meeting hosts will literally bring your campaign home to living rooms and community centers to meet their friends and recruit volunteers. What is your strategy to recruit them? Consider:

★ Family members
★ Close friends
★ Work colleagues
★ Political or nonprofit allies you've helped before
★ Key volunteers from networks in Community Inventory
★ Mavens who already host house meetings for others similar to you

3. Develop Your Finance Council

Starting with your finance chair, treasurer, and fund-raising
director, you need a team to raise the funds needed to win.
Who needs to be added to the finance council, and what is your
strategy to recruit them? Consider:

★ Finance chair

★ Treasurer

★ Fund-raising director

★ Current informal finance council

4. Choose Your Volunteer Corps Coordinators

Your best ambassadors and trainers, the volunteer corps
coordinators lead the people who form the backbone of
your campaign, strengthening and expanding your support.
Consider:

★ Volunteers in politics with close community ties

★ Opinion leaders who volunteer on campaigns like yours,
  already have good connections within the community, and
  have a Rolodex to help you recruit

★ House meeting hosts who want to take more responsibility
  within the campaign

★ Good teachers, trainers, nurturers

★ Techies who can set up basic data management systems so
  that as people enter the system, their areas of interest and
  levels of participation are all on file

5. Establish Your Election Protection Team

From voter registration to Election Day to recount, you must
have a council of voting experts and lawyers keeping an eye
on your votes at all times. You need a team with experience in
your community.

★ Appoint a campaign counsel

★ Add experts on election laws, voting rights, and campaigns

★ Include experienced activists for get-out-the-vote efforts in hot spots such as early voting, military ballots, and student voters

★ Use national networks with local chapters, hotlines, and other networks

PART III

MONEY

FIVE

Raise the Money

Your values are all in your checkbook.

ANN RICHARDS (1933–2006)

The late Ann Richards, former governor of Texas, provided this plainspoken advice at a women's networking lunch I attended in the 1990s: "I see a lot of nice handbags and purses in this room. Now if one of you ladies left this lunch and were hit by a car and someone opened your purse to find identification, they might look at your checkbook. What would they see? How would your spending priorities identify you?" She concluded: "Your values are all in your checkbook."

To attract people to your vision and plan, you must be able to appeal to their values, ask them for money, and receive it.

Whether you are seeking donations for political or philan-thropic efforts, you must believe in the purpose of your work and build the skills needed to ask others to help. Fund-raising in a down economy with intense competition for dollars is chal-lenging, but your call to service demands that you meet those challenges with new innovations in values-based fund-raising.

While many will be skeptical of a grassroots effort to raise and win against corporate cash, I am optimistic that small donor campaigns can still thrive. Yes, there are still very large donors, especially since the U.S. Supreme Court declared in *Citizens United* that corporations are people, but the Internet has democ-ratized fund-raising by giving people the tools to find each other

and to organize creatively in virtual space. The power of individuals to counter big money has been proven by grassroots campaigns that defeated better-funded candidates and initiatives.

Whether it's a political campaign, nonprofit, or NGO (nongovernmental organization), you should ask for money, goods,
and services. In tough economic times when cash is at a pre-
mium, many people are still hungry to participate and will give
or barter time, child care, space, food, coffee, legal and accounting services—all the things money can buy that people may
give. Scour your budget and see what your money is buying—
then make a finance plan where you plan to seek donations if
at all possible. Need space? Seek in-kind donated offices. Need
volunteers? Seek caregivers so parents can work the phones.
Need food? There are volunteers happy to cook for your team.
Need to fly? See if supporters can donate airline miles. There are
many people out there who want to join but don't have money
and don't know that you would appreciate services in lieu of
cash—don't miss a chance to empower them.

Your fund-raising pitch should cover the four forces of your
campaign: message, management, money, mobilization.

* **Message:** your values-based, authentic call to service and
  the vision, ideas, and values that will achieve the vision, and
  how you will gauge your progress.

* **Management:** your solid team of leaders and professionals
  with ethics, expertise, and experience, and how you measure
  their effectiveness.

* **Money:** a detailed campaign finance plan that explains how
  you will spend these donations and how you will track your
  budget. Your fund-raising is an expression of your message.
  If you are a homegrown campaign, the number or percentage of local donors is key. If you are trying to create an aura
  of invincibility, the sheer money figures may be what you
  highlight. If you are following the Occupy movement's
  Move Your Money agenda and chartering or moving your

political action committee with a local bank or credit union, say so.

* **Mobilization:** the volunteers and voters attracted to your mission, and how you keep them engaged and monitor the results. Include media in your ongoing efforts to cultivate a community of service around your mission and how you are measuring its growth and impact.

Political fund-raising entails a particular challenge because, unlike charitable donations, donors get no tax benefit for their campaign contributions. For campaign leaders and candidates, even the healthiest dose of personal ambition is insufficient to sustain the stamina necessary to spend several hours a day "dialing for dollars." You must keep your focus on the larger goal: the beauty of your dreams and the message you are sending to the future.

UNDERSTAND WHY PEOPLE GIVE

The most fundamental lesson in political fund-raising is understanding why people give. Most people give because they understand that money is necessary to win a campaign and achieve a vision, and they want to participate in an effort to create the kind of future they want to see for themselves, their families, their communities, and their society.

Many people tithe to their favorite charities, to local social enterprises, or to their place of worship. Others set aside a certain amount of money each year for political giving. Environmental advocate and Democratic National committeewoman Rachel Binah says, "Think of the money you give to charities and campaigns. What motivates you? Think of other people the same way—you just have to look beneath the surface."[1]

Do your research. Until you know what motivates potential donors, you cannot successfully attract their support. How will you know what attracts donors to causes? Ask them.

Your campaign begins with you and your closest circle of

family and friends, so your fund-raising should begin there too. I once saw the wife of a prominent candidate on a fund-raising tour. I asked if any of her close friends would be coming. "Oh we don't ask our friends for money," she declared. Really? Then why should we, the campaign supporters, ask our own friends for money? You can't hold back. If you are embarrassed to ask any of your friends for money, you will have a hard time asking me to ask mine.

Your Community Inventory and finance council plan have the names of people you know well and who know you. Begin by seeking donations from them; then grow your campaign from there. Your campaign leadership teams will discover information as the campaign goes along, and your outreach will adapt to include whatever you learn as you meet people and they interact with your campaign. Once you know why people give, you can tailor your requests to their needs and interests:

★ Some want to invest in a close friend because they believe in public service

★ Some want to support people who have supported them in the past

★ Some want to back a winner and think you have a good chance

★ Some can't stand your opponent

★ Some tithe a certain amount of money a year for particular causes, maybe yours

★ Some don't have time to volunteer but will invest in non-profits that do

★ Some do not want to give to political parties or nonprofits but only to individuals or tailored projects where they can see their money at work

Apply your research wisely by appealing to the reason donors give, so that with every call you are making a personal connection between your vision and the donor's vision.

BE WILLING TO ASK FOR MONEY

You have accepted your call to service, you work hard with your management team, you believe in your message, and you have a great plan to mobilize support. All you need is money to make it happen—just like entrepreneurs and innovators.

Those new to running for office or leading causes "shy away from fund-raising, feeling that it would make them appear too 'slick' and detract from their grassroots approach," says Dotty LeMieux. "They need to learn that money is a necessary evil to get their message out to the voters. They don't have to have the most money, but they do need enough to be viable."[2]

"Asking for money for yourself is a measure of what you think of yourself," says Rachel Binah. Some people, like the candidate's spouse who did not ask her friends for money, want to keep the personal and the political separate. Others are scared of rejection and would rather not call. But if you are going to do the work, you have to make the ask. Unless and until there are publicly financed campaigns, you will have to raise funds in a multi-billion dollar message environment and use creativity and frugality to leverage your resources.

Binah has participated in environmental and political friend-raising and fund-raising for decades. She advises, "Ask people, even if you don't think they have money." She recalls raising money for a Women Making History lunch in San Francisco supporting Barbara Boxer's first senate campaign. "It cost $150 to attend [and we] would have to travel several hours in each direction to go to it. I asked everyone I could think of to come. A woman heard about it and was upset that I hadn't asked her. I thought she was poor. But her mother had died and left her some money, and she wanted to spend it on Barbara Boxer. This woman continued to donate money for each campaign thereafter."

Finally, Binah urges, "Ask people who are always asked. They are the ones who always give. Don't let them off the hook because you want to protect them. Don't say. . . . 'Oh, I can't ask them, because they're always asked, and they always donate to everything.' That's what you want!"[3]

OFFER A VARIETY
OF FUND-RAISING OPPORTUNITIES

The most effective fund-raising networks are like menus in Chinese restaurants—opportunities offered a la carte rather than prix fixe offerings. In practical terms that means setting up a donation network offering tiered membership (with incentives such as monthly newsletters, discounts on events, having coffee with opinion leaders) as well as an open architecture that allows new people to come and go. This is the model favored by the Bay Area Democrats network that has conducted events in the San Francisco area for over ten years and raised early money for President Barack Obama. Cofounded by Wade Randlett and run by Marjan Philhour, the group is loosely organized, easily connected, with little command and control. "Committed Democrats were distressed at first that we did not endorse candidates or require mandatory membership," says Randlett. "But over time they came to enjoy the Chinese menu. We said 'Come as you are when you like.' Over ten years we have had 200 candidates—almost all federal—appearing at 125 to 150 candidate fund-raisers as well as countless meet-and-greets. . . . When the President came to San Francisco in April [2011], we had over 300 people give between $25 and $35,000. That is the broad base of our network."[4]

CREATE A MODEL OF SUSTAINABILITY

Donors looking for results need to see what you did with their money. The more people see their money in action, the more likely they are to keep the virtuous circle going. Using the Bay Area Democrats model,

★ Establish a platform and membership combination so you will have the ongoing funds for newsletters, events, and database maintenance

★ Create a management architecture that fits today's crowd-sourced, values-based politics

★ Stay connected to your base of donors to keep your campaign competitive and your doors open

★ Include donors who have already maxed out as well as new people

★ Show how you adapted your program based upon what you learned

★ Make sure your fund-raising director keeps your database current and your finance council members are aware of all ongoing events

Don't assume that because you do good work you will get money or that your dynamism alone will yield dollars. Not in this economy. People are looking at sustainable models such as CREDO mobile (formerly Working Assets), which runs a cell phone company and dedicates the profits to progressive infrastructure projects from children's welfare to voting rights.

MAP OUT YOUR CAMPAIGN FUND-RAISING PLAN

Good campaign fund-raising begins with a comprehensive finance plan, not unlike a start-up's business plan to raise venture capital. The following seven steps lead to a good campaign finance plan:

1. Forecast how much money you need to win. Begin with your message box, Community Inventory, campaign plan, campaign budget, and leadership teams exercises in hand as you plug in your resources. Your campaign calendar shows you when you need to raise the money, and your campaign budget lays out the dollar amounts and percentages to be spent on the message, management, money, and mobilization needed to win. Now consider information from your finance and research teams as to what past campaigns have raised for this position. Using these figures as a guideline, start setting some fund-raising goals. Are you in the ballpark? Make sure you plan to get the money by the time you want to spend it. Let's say for example that you are running for mayor and you have to raise a million dollars by Labor Day of 2012. You know the million-dollar figure comes from the cost of contacting 250,000 voters, holding 100 house meetings, posting lawn signs, and establishing a social network by and for your beehive of supporters. And you know you must go on TV by August so people know you. That's your plan, you know people with money, you know mavens who influence giving—so now your campaign finance plan puts that money where your mouth is.

2. Establish control mechanisms. Check with an attorney so that you know who can give how much money to your race. There may be individual and PAC donation limits for a primary and general election, or overall limits on local, state, or federal giving. Also, decide whether to avoid certain sources of funds. Some candidates decide early on that they will decline money from certain industries (such as tobacco) or from any political action committees.

Both Democrats and Republicans have learned the hard way that your internal controls must include staffers who check each other's work. New York mayor Michael Bloomberg made a contribution for "ballot security measures" (a controversial method by which operatives check voter registration and identification status) only to find after his check was cashed and his re-election well over that the recipient purchased a house instead of a campaign operation.[5] On the Democratic side, dozens of California legislators and party committees were robbed by "the Bernie Madoff of campaign treasurers" who bilked dozens of campaigns out of millions of dollars.[6]

Jennifer Crider, deputy director of the Democratic Congressional Campaign Committee, advises campaigns to assign a staffer to compare bank records with campaign filings every month. As a former bank employee, Crider knows how to read bank statements and catch discrepancies and recommends that all campaigns protect themselves from intentional or unintentional errors. "It's not just campaign fund-raising, it's campaign spending, campaign reporting, and campaign reconciling of spending and reporting that will keep you on top of your finances," she advises.

Draw ethical lines, and figure out other sources. In our mayor example, let's say you refuse money from people with city hall contracts. Now that's cash from the Community Inventory and finance council that is off limits. Are you sure this is your message? There is no turning back, or asking their spouses to give, or limiting only certain kinds of contractors. If this is your pledge, make it and keep it. Then cross potential givers off the list and keep searching.

For example, a teacher with Close-Up Foundation described how his chapter was fund-raising to send kids to Washington and wrestled with receiving funds offered from a local franchisee of a major alcohol company. Though they needed the money, they decided that if alcohol wasn't legal for the kids to drink, it wasn't appropriate to fund their trip.

The entire leadership team—the steering committee, the staff, the volunteers—must all know what's in and out of bounds. If you are running for partisan political office, the political party committees will likely train your team in best practices so that you have specific templates to use.

You must vet and process all potential donations to be sure they comply with the legal and ethical lines you have drawn. This means having your finance chair and fund-raising director work with the research team to look up any reports of activity both positive and controversial. This also means having a computer data entry system to receive contributions as well as a fund-raising page such as ActBlue. These controls will facilitate your ongoing fund-raising efforts as well as your campaign finance reporting. Purchase software or services needed to track past and potential contributors and to prepare campaign finance filing reports.

3. Decide if your campaign will borrow money. The question of going into debt is a personal one for candidates and family. Think through these options at the start of a campaign rather than wait until the end. Are you willing to borrow money? Can you give yourself a loan? Would you mortgage your house to win? Would you sacrifice retirement dreams to achieve your vision?

One candidate from a rural area had lackluster fund-raising numbers and was hesitant about taking out a loan to help fund his campaign. He was advised by political colleagues if he went all in, they would help fund-raise. A Democratic leader told him, "You own a farm. Bet the farm." He did—literally—and won.

4. Identify your prospective donors. Your boot camp exercises have laid out your potential donors: now identify them on your campaign finance plan. Pull out your personal Rolodex or holiday card list of family and friends. Start with their names and affiliations. Then branch out to your Community Inventory (see chapter 3), and prepare a list of people you know from those political and social networks.

Review the latest annual reports of local cultural institutions, civic organizations, and nonprofits to refresh information on the giving patterns of your community's philanthropists from your Community Inventory. Many Internet sites, starting with the Federal Election Commission (FEC), post donor lists that include the donor's name, contribution amount, occupation, employer, and address. FEC lists are available to the public at www.fec .gov/. Most state and local election offices also maintain lists of political donors. If someone just gave to your opponents, you will want to know that before you call.

You'll want to update your Community Inventory and financial plans as often as you can. A friend recently told me he got a call from a candidate the day after he did an event for her primary opponent. He was quite impressed that she knew about his event and that she called him directly to make a case for him to reconsider and also support her. Eventually he did.

Although you or your team can legally research any individual's history of political contributions, what you do with that information depends on your ethics. Use it to determine a donor's ability to give, not to spam everyone on a list for a donation. Instead, ask prominent people who support you to write a letter or solicitation to their supporters endorsing you as a candidate. Also ask for their permission to post such letters or endorsements on your Web site. Each call should direct people back to your Web site so they can see that there is a large community of support.

Do not seek support in a vacuum. Peer-to-peer networking is essential to fund-raising. Although you must make a personal appeal, you must also reinforce your ask with a peer-to-peer communication from someone among your campaign's teams of kitchen cabinet, house meeting hosts, election protection team, finance council, or volunteer corps coordinators. One-on-one communication is always the best.

5. Identify your available communications tools. There are a variety of fund-raising tools you will need; you must outline each of them, including candidate call time, personal meetings and events, phone banks, direct mail, and e-mail. Many cool new tools may come along, but the essence is the same—you have to sit and take the time to call for money. The more technology that crowds our lives, the more important a personal touch becomes.

6. Match up donors with tools and targeted dollars. Review your prospective donors. How will you approach them? By holding a reception? Making a simple phone call? If possible, phoning is always the best way because you do not incur overhead costs associated with fund-raising events. (Texting is cheaper, but be judicious in its use and check the law first.)

Then chart out the donors, the communications tools, and the targeted dollars to be raised. If you are telephoning, create a call sheet—a record that contains a potential donor's brief bio and contribution history—for each donor you intend to call on any given day. If your call sheet about a donor includes her work for women's groups, stress the female candidate or women-in-campaign-leadership role, women's group endorsements, and any news on relevant policies.

7. Prepare a fund-raising kit for potential donors. Your kit should include a résumé or candidate biography with a clear explanation of your call to service, vision for the future, big ideas, and values to achieve the vision. You also need a copy of the campaign plan, the fund-raising plan, and any recent polling or articles about the race, as well as a list of your endorsements, some campaign literature, and photographs. If you work with a nonprofit, include profiles on the people you help and testimonials. If you work with a candidate, provide the candidate's photo so that people can see whom they are supporting.

Encourage potential donors to follow their money. Update your Web site with volunteer and service activities. Identify where you will officially report donations: political campaigns file with elections boards, and nonprofits file with the Internal Revenue Service. Many activists look over the IRS 990 forms to see how the money is being spent. When the San Francisco Giants Community Fund Board on which I serve looks at awarding grants in violence prevention, health, and education, we research how the money is to be used and whether it will be advertised to the charity's constituency. Our grant applications include opportunities for people to say whether they will mention the grant in a newsletter, by e-mail, or on a Web site so that our donors can track their dollars through to the recipients they serve. So if we raise funds via Until There's a Cure Night and promise the money to a set of grantees, the fans that support Jr. Giants can go to each grantee's Web site and see their dollars in action.

★ ★ ★ ★ ★ ★ ★ ★ ★ ★ ★ ★ ★

ASKING FOR MONEY:
HIGH-TECH MEETS HIGH TOUCH

"The key is donor's choice," says Brian Wolff, former executive director of the Democratic Congressional Campaign Committee with over a dozen years' experience in national fund-raising for campaigns ranging from Congress to the presidency. "If donors feel empowered by the information you give them about your candidacy or cause, they usually become investors."

Wolff offers five elements to consider when asking for money.

1. Leverage network effects. Asking for and receiving funds is the single most important indicator of support for a campaign—it proves that people believe in your cause/campaign. Money attracts money; the more people who invest in you, the more people who will be willing to invest in you.

2. Share information strategically. Keeping your investors (donors) informed is hugely important. Post and e-mail progress reports. You never know when your report will spur them to write another check or offer another idea.

3. Crowd-source ideas. Your donors are intellectual resources, not just bank accounts. Look to this base for ideas when you need expertise on the issues.

4. Activate your friends-and-family network. This network can exponentially increase your universe by reaching out as real ambassadors for your campaign.

5. Stay personal. The more personal you can keep your communications, the better. It shows respect and that you take responsibility for making the ask directly. In these days of the Internet and real-time technology, the handwritten note never goes unnoticed.

Source: Brian Wolff, e-mail, May 20, 2007.

VARY YOUR FUND-RAISING TOOLS

Dialing for dollars. To set up an afternoon of call time, gather the day's call sheets, your fund-raising kit, any up-to-date news, the latest polling figures, water, and snacks.

Staffers should prepare by calling potential givers or their assistants to make sure they are in the office that day or reachable by cell phone. Send a fax or e-mail ahead of the call regarding a specific event or poll or other significant information that will be the topic of the call. For inspiration you may want to have photographs of the people being helped by your nonprofit or cause. Candidates may want to send a family photo or pictures of people from the campaign trail whom they are seeking the opportunity to serve.

Assign someone to sit with the candidate or director to dial the numbers and get through other assistants to fund-raising contacts before placing the candidate on the phone. This saves time, as you can have a staffer setting up one call while the candidate is wrapping up another. Be sure to take notes so that you have a record of what people are saying for further action and follow-up. Schedule what you know will be longer conversations toward the end of the session so they don't take up the entire time.

You should ask for a *specific* contribution. If you ask for support, the person may agree and send you a check for $25. If you want $500, then ask for it: tell the person that you are preparing your budget for mailing and need to know whether you can count on $500 from her. Then *pause*. Anticipate silence—do not rush to fill it, especially not by lowering the amount requested. Drink your water if necessary. Let your request stand, and respect the donor's need to think before committing.

Receiving a contribution feels great. "It's like getting a scholarship," says longtime political fund-raiser Brian Wolff. "Someone believes that you have a future and is investing in you."[7]

Savor the moment—put the name on a donor's chart, give yourself a quick high five—then move on with the next call. To keep your spirits up, intersperse calls to people who are more likely to give with those less likely donors. If you get a large commitment, leverage it to sway other callers, not just with a positive attitude but with specific inspiration to join in a success: "Ms. Smith just gave us $500 for the printing of the mailer; will you invest in the stamps?"

Once you get a commitment, write a thank-you note to the contributor for her promise of $500 to the cause. If the person requests additional information, fax it immediately, and place her call sheet in a stack to call again the following day.

Call and ask for more money from people who have already donated. If they say no, then ask them to host a house meeting or to identify five other people whom you should call.

Remember: ask for specific amounts, be firm with people who have pledged to contribute, and set aside enough time to make calls. Give your volunteers call sheets, a general script, and practice making calls. Put a resource person in the room to support callers. Celebrate successes. Keep snacks within reach. Make verbal and written thank-yous a priority!

Meetings and events. Sometimes you need in-person meetings to secure individual contributions. As during phone calls, have updated information in your fund-raising kit, know the donor's political and giving history, ask for a specific amount, respect the pause—drink that water to stop yourself from answering your own question or lowering your request—and, as always, listen and say thank you.

Events bring people together to see the candidate, get a campaign update, and invest in the values, ideas, and vision of the campaign. They can also cost a lot unless you plan wisely. Some campaigns use the house-meeting model for small-donor fund-raising. For example, congressman Chris Murphy of Connecticut attended over sixty house parties where he recruited campaign donors and volunteers. Hosts invited guests to attend for free; after hearing the message, some wrote checks, some enlisted as volunteers, and others opted to host future events. By giving people the opportunity to experience his campaign up close, Murphy expanded his network and attracted the support—and dollars—to win.[8]

Phone banks. A phone bank is a place where a group of people sit and make calls. Nowadays people can call from home on their cell phones, even using their laptops for a predictive dialer that connects the call from their laptop to their phone. Use a phone bank to follow up on mailed invitations to increase event attendance. A call reminds prospects about the event and greatly increases the likelihood that they will buy a ticket and attend. Also, if prospects cannot attend, ask them for a contribution. Once a donor has pledged by phone, send a confirmation stating the exact amount. Use phone banks to collect on pledges following in-person and phone solicitations.

Direct mail solicitation. Direct mail, or campaign promotion through the U.S. postal service, includes two types of fundraising: resolicitation of your campaign's donor file and cold prospecting. Experts estimate that donor resolicitation provides close to 80 percent of the net income from a direct mail campaign, whereas cold prospecting for new donors may cost more than it delivers in contributions. But its goal is to acquire new donors to resolicit several times before the campaign ends.

Before embarking on an expensive and high-risk prospecting venture, consider whether the campaign has the expertise in house to run a prospecting program; whether the campaign can afford to hire a mail consultant; whether there is a large enough potential universe of prospects who would be interested in the campaign to make a professional prospecting program economical in the short-term and profitable in the long-term; and whether the campaign has time to implement a successful direct mail program.

Logistically, your next step is production and printing: prepare and proofread the letter, envelope, and business reply envelope so that they are ready for the printer; decide how the campaign will mail the solicitation (through volunteers or a mail shop); and identify a good union printer that can meet the campaign's deadlines at a good price.

Before you print, remember: you get what you *inspect* not what you *expect*. Ask several other people to proofread the copy. Then proofread your mailer again after printing. A candidate for state attorney general once printed up thousands of postcards for voters introducing himself as a "compatet" attorney. Luckily, a *competent* staffer caught the error, and his team spent the day shredding, instead of stamping, the doomed mailers.

Record the basic facts about each piece of mail accurately so that you can evaluate the results. A tracking system should include the following:

★ date mailed

★ package code (if different mailings go out to the same list)

★ number of pieces mailed

★ number of contributors (daily and running totals)

★ the total amount contributed (daily and running totals)

★ percentage return (number of contributors divided by number mailed)

★ average contribution

★ dollar return per thousand mailed

★ cost of mailing, per thousand

This data will allow you to compare the results of different prospect mailings to determine which lists were more successful and what message copy was most effective.

Online fund-raising. The low administrative costs of Internet-based fund-raising can yield high returns if you plan correctly and execute securely. Take credit card payments online: a credit card donation is money in the bank. Purchase software or services from your Web designer or the bank handling your campaign account. Many progressive campaigns use ActBlue.com to set up accounts and run all the funding through that server at great convenience to campaign operations.

Remember the campaign's Internet protocols: that friend-raising comes before fund-raising. Use your donation lists for campaign and reporting only, and protect your Web systems from spyware and viruses. Using cloud computing will help eliminate the need for major in-house software purchases, allowing savings and efficiency. Here are some tips for successful online fund-raising.

* **Present your vision to your audience.** When composing e-mails, visualize your audience, write in your own voice, communicate simply and directly, and provide links to helpful information. Ask recipients to forward your message to their friends and family. Your credibility is key: be accurate and link to a trusted Web resource for verification.

* **Send your e-mail to an already supportive audience.** If you are growing your list, do not start by asking for money— ask an ambassador to circulate your message. For example, former Senator Max Cleland, a hero of the Vietnam War, sent an e-mail with the subject line "Send a Marine to Congress" to veterans and military families across the country. That e-mail helped raise the national profile—and the campaign coffers—of candidate Paul Hackett in Ohio's Second Congressional District among those who knew of and trusted Senator Cleland.

* **Detail the value of the contribution precisely.** A $10,000 goal seems like a vast sum of money going into the nowhere land of a campaign treasury. But $10,000 that represents 100 rental vans to get out the vote, 1,000 volunteer meals, 2,500 signs, or 5,000 bumper stickers is a precise goal.

* ★ **Showcase your supporters' success.** Fill a thermometer, a ruler, a baseball bat (popularized by Governor Howard Dean), a chili pepper (Governor Bill Richardson's choice), or some other graphic that changes with each donation. Choose graphics that depict your candidate's mission and measure success.

* ★ **Track your readers and responses.** A good e-mail vendor will have statistics on when people tend to open mail and how many open yours, click on your links, or give through a solicitation. This accounting is crucial in determining your success.

* ★ **Ask readers to act and report on their actions.** Your e-mails must captivate your audience. Crowd-source creative action items—for example, signing a petition, contributing to a specific campaign event, blanketing a community with signs, or hosting a house meeting on a given night.

* ★ **Format for success.** Remember that many people access e-mail via tablets or smart phones, so you must test each message for small formats. Some users receive only text; their mobile settings block hyperlinks and image files so as to speed up e-mail access. So do not get fancy in your formatting. Most requests follow this pattern:

Subject line: Make a direct request that is not cryptic, possibly clever. Think 140-character tweet length.

Dear _____ (First Name)

50 words with a link to action on your Web site

50 more words with another link to the same action on your Web site

Closing message or tagline of campaign (140 characters maximum)

Signature signoff with your name and a link to the same action on your Web site

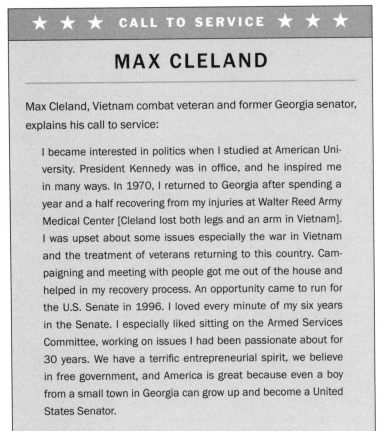

★ ★ ★ CALL TO SERVICE ★ ★ ★

MAX CLELAND

Max Cleland, Vietnam combat veteran and former Georgia senator, explains his call to service:

I became interested in politics when I studied at American University. President Kennedy was in office, and he inspired me in many ways. In 1970, I returned to Georgia after spending a year and a half recovering from my injuries at Walter Reed Army Medical Center [Cleland lost both legs and an arm in Vietnam]. I was upset about some issues especially the war in Vietnam and the treatment of veterans returning to this country. Campaigning and meeting with people got me out of the house and helped in my recovery process. An opportunity came to run for the U.S. Senate in 1996. I loved every minute of my six years in the Senate. I especially liked sitting on the Armed Services Committee, working on issues I had been passionate about for 30 years. We have a terrific entrepreneurial spirit, we believe in free government, and America is great because even a boy from a small town in Georgia can grow up and become a United States Senator.

Source: Max Cleland, "Wireside Chat," *Trail Mix*, April 30, 2006.

Apply the same high campaign code of conduct to e-mail as to every other communication. Potential supporters, reporters, and your opposition are receiving these e-mails. Say nothing online that you would not authorize someone to say off-line or in person.

BE DILIGENT ABOUT FINANCE REPORTING

Candidates and leaders of nonprofits should familiarize themselves with all financial filings, compliance exercises, and governance processes before they form their finance council. Finance reports are legal documents. Treat them with care. Do not file false, incomplete, or controversial finance reports. If your board of directors or kitchen cabinet includes a qualified attorney, enlist that person early in the process to make sure that you meet all the public requirements. Recruit someone you trust to act as treasurer with responsibility for filing all the campaign finance reports required under city, county, state, and federal laws. Ask a third party with trusted judgment to review your finance reports before your treasurer files them. This person should double-check to confirm that you have not accepted money from a disreputable individual or organization.

Keep in mind that the press and your competitors will look at your quarterly reports to see what shape you are in. *Your fund-raising must match your message, your campaign budget, and finance plan.* For example, if you are raising funds to effect change in a community, your donors should mostly live in that community. If the community is poor, the large number of donors should compensate for the small size of contributions.

Comply with the elections regulations. Confusion over intricacies of the laws and filing mistakes can lead to embarrassing fines, negative press coverage, and an issue your opponent can attack. Follow these best practices:

★ Get a lawyer.
★ Get all advice in writing from your lawyer and from any relevant entities such as the FEC, IRS, or state agencies.
★ Know the regulations and filing deadlines and put them on your campaign calendar.
★ Procure computer software or reporting services that enable you to produce reports quickly and accurately. Tech companies may be inclined to make in-kind contributions of services in lieu of cash. If that is legal, take them and report them.
★ Cross-check bank statements with filing reports.

★ Entrust at least one person with maintaining full compliance
   with the law.
★ Check the relevant government Web sites regularly for
   updates.

The run-up to any filing deadline adds pressure. Stick to your
campaign policy or your management and internal controls.
Watchdogs look closely, so see whether reports are filed accurately.

Finally, vet and research any contributions well before the
deadline. No one reads your campaign filings more closely than
your opponent!

★ ★ ★

**GET REAL:
PREPARE A FUND-RAISING PLAN**

1. Establish Budget Goals, Controls, and Plans

★ Forecast the budget, starting with what past campaigns have
   raised for this cause.
★ Check with an attorney so that you know who can give how
   much money.
★ Decide what kind of money you will raise and from whom.
   Are there sources of funds you will avoid?
★ Establish management and internal controls to vet and process all potential donations to facilitate your ongoing fund-
   raising efforts as well as your campaign finance reporting.
★ Map out your campaign plan and projected dollars (and
   percentages) to be spent on the management, message,
   money, media, and mobilization needed to win.

Be sure to highlight items you can get donated as opposed to
purchased.

2. Identify Your Prospective Donors

★ You: Are you willing to borrow money? Can you give
   yourself a loan? Would you mortgage your house in order
   to win?

★ List your family and friends.

★ List your peers from high school, college, or professional school; coworkers from any jobs or volunteer positions held; people to whom you have donated political or charitable contributions.

★ Consider your opponent's record and any political antagonists who might fund you.

★ Consider people who tend to give to elected officials. Will any current or former officeholders contact their networks for you?

3. Identify Your Available Tools

★ Candidate call time

★ Phone banks

★ Personal meetings and events

★ Direct mail

★ E-mail

4. Match Up Donors with Tools and Targeted Dollars

Review your prospective donors and think about the best way to approach the sources on your list. Then chart out the donors, the tools, and the targeted dollars to be raised. (See table on next page.)

Donors	Tools	Targeted Dollars
You	Bank Loan	
Family	Call/Meetings/Events	
Friends	Call/Meeting/Events/ E-mail	
School Alums	Phone Banks/Meetings	
Peers	Events/Direct Mail/E-mail	
Community Leaders	Call Time/Meetings/ Events/E-mail	
People You Have Supported	Call Time/Meetings/ Events/E-mail	

PART IV

MOBILIZATION

SIX

★ ★ ★

Connect with People

Just so we're reminded of the ones who are held back,
Up front there oughta' be a Man in Black.

JOHNNY CASH

Every communication must deliver your message to head and heart. Some people speak better to America's head, and others to her heart. Only the best communicators speak to both, literally wearing the colors of the people and connecting with their dreams as Johnny Cash did.

Most Americans spend only a few minutes of their week thinking about politics and public policy, so you compete with the million other messages from TV, radio, Web sites, and mailboxes. To fit your message into a sliver of attention, you must cast it in their language, not yours, and repeat it.

People must see you in the job to determine whether you can do it. Give interviews, do town hall meetings, attend debates—do whatever you can to "interview" for the job.

If you are volunteering, appear on behalf of your cause or your candidate at community forums, house meetings, and debates. If you are running for office, create opportunities to address the media as a leader in your community so that people can see you as part of the official family.

PREPARE FOR EVERY PERFORMANCE

"Proper preparation prevents poor performance," was my mom's theory of school homework. The greatest sign of respect is your level of advance work before any public appearance.

Dress rehearsal. Every event is a job interview. Your dress must match your message. Dress professionally, but appropriately for the audience. Consider how your clothing might reinforce your message or your character. Ask your hosts whether you need to avoid certain colors, add a head covering such as a yarmulke or scarf, avoid poses like crossing your legs to reveal the soles of your shoes. Don't wear your fancy suit to a low-income neighborhood. Don't wear wingtips to a ballpark. Avoid distracting patterns and strong perfume or cologne. The late Ann Richards told women "no dangly earrings." Avoid flip-flops (the footwear and the policy switches). Proper dress and grooming communicate respect for both your hosts and your cause.

Young people especially should dress for campaigning, not for clubbing. A young mother came up to me at a summer 2011 boot camp and said, "We need to have the talk with these young people. I make sure my sons are dressed for the occasion and it shocks us to sit next to young leaders in shorts." So here's the talk: wear something closer to a dress suit than a bathing suit when you represent your community at conferences and events. Young Democrats of America President Rod Snyder and Executive Vice President Colmon Eldridge told me that they made a joint decision to always attend YDA conferences in a coat and tie so as to always convey a sense of professionalism and leadership.

Some people add a signature touch that audiences come to expect: for New York senator Daniel Patrick Moynihan it was the bow tie that reinforced his intellectual side, for U.S. Secretary of State Hillary Clinton it is the two-piece suit that reinforces her feminist "Sisterhood of the Traveling Pants Suits."

Examine your personal habits, and ask your kitchen cabinet

to do the same. Do you forget basic manners, like saying please and thank you? Do you avoid eye contact when talking with people? Do you fidget, smoke, or bite your nails in public? Do you repeat certain words and phrases, such as "you know" or "to tell the truth"? Such habits may reveal a lack of confidence. Break them. Use a smartphone to record yourself practicing a speech. Watch it. Note your strengths and weaknesses. Watch your posture, keep your hands close to the table or podium, and *breathe* while answering a question.

Many candidates will be asked to sample local flavor—pork chop on a stick, batter-fried Twinkies, or homemade firehouse chili. Don't drink more than a glass of alcohol and never drink and drive. I loved the deep fried Oreos in Wisconsin but have yet to see a candidate look dignified while eating a foot-long corn dog. Remember how your eating will look on camera—think Rick Perry swallowing a corn dog or John Kerry nibbling a cheesesteak—because your foes will make a meal out of yours. Even if you are not competing on the national stage serving up fodder for late night comics, remember that YouTube is global.

Deliver your message. When you speak for your cause, always start by making your pitch. Be clear, using language customized to the audience as Drs. Luntz and Lakoff teach. Be concise, using no more than seventy-five words to convey your message. Be consistent, repeating your values. Be convincing by linking an issue to a value with a personal story with morals that evoke your political principles. Be humble: ask people to vote for you or your cause and thank them for their consideration.

Give people a reason to join you. Articulate your call to service, invite people to be part of something bigger, and explain how you can win together. Convey your qualifications by connecting with your audience and leveraging endorsements by individuals, organizations, and networks from your Community Inventory.

Know the show. When I commended a man about his dad's appearance on the *Daily Show,* he laughed and said, "The minute I

★ ★ ★ CALL TO SERVICE ★ ★ ★

FRED ROSS

Fred Ross Jr. heard his call to service through the work of his father, Fred Ross Sr., and United Farm Workers of America president César Chavez. Ross recalls: "I grew up in a household where fighting injustice was a way of life, from my father's tireless organizing in the barrios and fields to my mother's, Frances Ross's, pioneering work with the mentally ill." In 1964 Fred Ross Sr. organized Yaqui Indian and Mexican American families in Guadalupe, Arizona, for "the simplest justice: paved streets, traffic lights on a dangerous two-lane highway, and basic services that other communities took for granted," recalls Ross Jr.

> One night, after 897 residents had registered to vote, the newly formed Guadalupe Organization (GO) held its first town meeting. What I saw that night was a classic example of how people organize, build power, and hold elected officials accountable. I saw it in the faces and voices of men and women who had never spoken publicly before [who] got up and peppered the candidates with tough questions. That experience made me immensely proud of my father, seeing how an organizer changes lives and gives people the tools to build power and win justice.

> I learned from César Chavez and my father that the organizer works quietly behind the scenes, patiently asking questions, listening respectfully, agitating, teaching new leaders, pushing them to take action and create hope *con animo*, "with great enthusiasm."

Source: Excerpted from Fred Ross, foreword to *Cesar Chavez: Autobiography of La Causa*, by Jacques E. Levy (Minneapolis: University of Minnesota Press, 2007), reprinted by permission of the University of Minnesota Press.

found out he was scheduled, I said, 'Dad have you seen the show? Do you know that he's going to be making fun? You have to get ready.' Everything went great because my father had prepared."

Anytime you go on TV, research first. If this is *Hardball*, expect a tough pitch from Chris Matthews. If this is Keith Olbermann on Friday, you're appearing before his reading of Thurber. If it is FOX, anticipate Greta van Susteren's cross-examination skills. Every host has a style. Know it.

Watch your opponents' appearances, too. Study their mannerisms and their dress code. Review your competitive intelligence on your opponents' messages and your media hosts' past coverage of your issues.

If you are going on radio, listen to the show in advance. "People who make references to our features got extra points in our book," says comedian and commentator Will Durst, cohost of the *Will and Willie Show* in San Francisco. "We talk about guests before and after they are on the show, so it helps their cause to show us and the audience that they were listening before they came on." Avoid telling jokes, even if you think you are funny. "Remember," cautions Durst, "we are the comics— not you. Voters appreciate intentional humor from professional comedians, not unintentional humor from amateur politicians."[1]

Before getting into the meat of an interview, many hosts break the ice with their favorite topic, so you should know what it is. My frequent radio visits to the Jon Elliott show often begin with baseball, as my San Francisco Giants and his San Diego Padres are rivals. If you don't know the host, practice with someone imitating him or her so you can be ready. You get one chance for your pitch before the host starts in on you so make it count.

For those about to blog, know that audience too. The *Huffington Post* has now merged with AOL, creating even more platforms for interconnectivity. The tone has changed as well: features on *Third World America* (the title of blog founder Arianna Huffington's book) and efforts to help the middle class are cast "beyond left and right." Know before you go that when you post, the audience is primed to see whether you understand the ethos of the site.

The microphone is always on. Someone's camera is always rolling. No matter where you are, stay on message. Avoid microphone chatter, off-the-cuff comments, and insults. In 2006, former senator George Allen used the term *macaca* to describe a young man of Indian descent tracking Allen's campaign movements with a video camera. The young man made a vlog (a video blog) of Allen's slur, and Allen's opponents sent that moment virally into the mainstream media spotlight. Allen never fully apologized and lost to Democrat Jim Webb.[2] Now that Allen is running again in 2012, his "macaca moment" is sure to be remembered.

You are always on. "Once you are on, you are on," says Andrea Dew Steele, founder of Emerge America, a grassroots women's training network. Steele tells aspiring women leaders, "You are the leader no matter where you are."[3] When you are picking up dry cleaning, shopping for food, or chasing your kids through a park, you are on. Driving with a bumper sticker makes you an ambassador for the candidate or cause. You don't want to lose votes by cutting off other drivers or careening down the highway. People will constantly measure how you relate to the public, potential donors, reporters, and volunteers.

If you are running to be first among equals to represent your peers within your political party, people will look to see if you can be an effective ambassador for them at the national level. If for example, like thousands of others, you make your first run for office as a delegate to a national presidential nominating convention, you will be meeting with other supporters of the candidate and will want to present yourself as the best local ambassador of a national campaign. We saw this in action at an exciting March 2008 California Democratic Party convention boot camp where aspiring delegates got up to practice their pitches for Barack Obama or Hillary Clinton before hundreds of us. While, as expected, they each said something positive about their candidate, the best ones talked about a positive agenda for America, not about how much they wanted to beat the other side. Careful preparation makes you ready for prime time at this basic starting block of political office.

KEEP AN OPEN FEEDBACK LOOP

An effective public servant listens to what people are saying for both the good news, such as community support for candidates and causes, and bad news, such as discontent and in some cases outright rebellion. An open feedback loop means that you put information out to people, people respond with feedback, you process their feedback, you lock in positives and adjust negatives, and then you send information back out. With the kitchen cabinet, you will get the bad news one way or another. The challenge is to mechanize how feedback comes to you and how your reinforcements or rebuttals go back out.

A campaign worker is responsible for making sure that the feedback you receive on the phones or in the neighborhoods is reported to the campaign leadership, and that you get information you can bring back to voters. Campaigns should have feedback sheets to use after events or any kind of outreach so there is a sense of how the message is being heard and what responses people are getting in the community.

When you call your members, poll your voters, or convene community meetings with your neighbors, you won't always get what you expect to hear. Be prepared to listen. Use the message-box technique to help figure out where your message needs clarity and whether or not people are with you. Perhaps what people are saying about you is not what you anticipated before you called them. Perhaps your negatives are stronger than you thought.

Good listening works for candidates and causes. If, for instance, you are working with a nonprofit that decides to increase membership fees, your pledge drive might reveal angry people who do not want to pay the increase. In that case, you may have to step back, reflect on why the increase is needed, and do as much belt tightening as you can. Then go back to your members with a fuller explanation of how raising their fees was a last resort, taken after everyone involved with the nonprofit tightened their belts, and how raising their fees will ultimately result in a stronger nonprofit performing more effective public service.

The general rule is to reinforce or readjust as necessary and to make sure people know that you listened, you heard, and you responded respectfully.

DEVELOP YOUR MEDIA PLAN

Every campaign for a cause or a candidate needs a communications strategy that guides the nuts-and-bolts media plan for connecting with people and persuading them to support you.

A good *media plan* is a portfolio of free and paid-for media that attempts to schedule your paid media (mailers, radio spots, and television commercials) around your free media (press conferences and news coverage) so that people get double the exposure to your message through different media. For example, they receive your mailer on the same day that they see TV coverage of your press conference, or they pass your billboard at the same time that they hear you on a local radio drive-time talk show. Group free press activities into message weeks, or issue weeks, during which you communicate a particular piece of information to people.

A media plan requires a clear statement of your objectives: communicate the message to the people likely to support you, as many times as needed to reach a tipping point of support.

Arc of the narrative. Your campaign kickoff event introduces your message to people, and you emphasize different parts of this message to different people during the following weeks through free press events and message weeks. Paid-media advertising reminds people of your argument for progress. Then, in the final days of the campaign, your free and paid media should come together and make it clear to people that you have proved your argument. At the start, say what you are going to do (hold 100 house meetings, conduct a listening tour, visit every community, collect ten thousand signed petitions for your initiative). Then do it.

Strengths of the media. People must hear your message many times before they can absorb it. Your media plan will be more successful with five mail pieces than with a radio spot that airs only five times, yet the costs of each might be about the same. Moreover, few media institutions reach across the entire political bandwidth, and so you must communicate your message in different venues to reach everyone. Ethnic media are also crucial: for example, about half of Latino voters are under the age of forty, so if you want to attract these young voters and keep them engaged, your outreach must include Spanish-language messaging lest you miss a generation not only now, but for life.[4] Your Community Inventory should have revealed the dominant languages that your constituents speak, and that information should guide your non-English-language media planning.

Vary your communications tools to leverage the strengths of each medium and integrate all forms of media: broadcast television, cable television, videos in mobile format, radio, blogs, Web ads, newspapers, community weeklies, direct mail, billboards, and telephones. Keep in mind that the traditional outlets all have Internet presence.

Broadcast television. Broadcast television reaches millions of voters with a unified message, and reaching these numbers is critical in most large campaigns. If you have the money to dominate television, do it. Buying a few commercials is a waste of media money unless you make a small buy and combine it with a video to create buzz.

Cable television. Cable television provides benefits similar to broadcasting at less cost, and you can target your spending on stations that serve only viewers in your community. In fact, you can target specific neighborhoods according to their cable service. More and more campaigns purchase small cable ads, couple them with viral videos, and create stories about the reactions to the ads. Web sites like spotcable.com will tell you exactly what cable channels run in each community—much like a TV channel menu in a hotel room—and sell you ads to reach your voters on the shows they watch so you can pinpoint buys accordingly.

A note about television programming: many young people watch television online, so to reach them you will need to purchase Web ads streaming on sites like Hulu.

Video. Post videos of your presentations on your Web site as a video résumé. If you are working with a cause, include your members giving testimonials (e.g., "Why I joined the union," "Why I am fighting for universal health care," "My personal commitment to fight global warming," or "Why my family will benefit from stem cell research"). If you are working with a campaign, your video should spotlight volunteers and supporters of an issue or candidate (e.g., "Why my family supports this school bond" or "Why as a veteran I am endorsing this candidate for office").

Keep it real—the more personal the better. Include personal appeals on your donations page from a nonprofit board member, pledge drive chair, or candidate. Cross-post in as many venues as possible (YouTube, etc.), and keep a full video inventory of your public service.

Mobile format. Make sure your video plays on mobile devices like cell phones and iPads since that's where most people would watch them. The Anna Eshoo "Challenge the Sacred Cows" video on VHS format from 1988 was innovative for its time. Now campaigns create a Web platform capable of sending messages viral and connecting to the beehive of interdependent thinkers and innovators. I am far more likely to forward a text message with your video than I am to watch it on a laptop sometime in the future. The instant buzz around mobile devices is far more nimble and effective.

As you embrace technology, also accept that technology is capturing you: the simplest cell-phone camera can record everything you say or do. Live accordingly. Accept that someone will record your movements for posterity and be polite to your trackers (videographers sent by the opposition) to avoid "macaca moments."

Radio. Radio is an extremely cost-effective medium by which to connect with people. Syndicated radio host Bill Press observes: "Fewer and fewer people read newspapers or watch TV news. Especially for politically active people, talk radio has a huge influence on what people think and how people vote. It also presents a huge opportunity for influencing public opinion, building public awareness and support, getting the message out, getting people to participate."[5]

A good media plan has a strategy for radio that includes ads, audio releases, and live airtime.

Radio advertisements. Check your local listings as well as national talk show resources like Talkers.com (the Web site of *Talkers* magazine) to determine which ones to target. Talkers .com posts radio content and audience information in online features such as The Talkers Ten (the top weekly topics), The Heavy Hundred (the 100 most important radio talk show hosts in America), and The Top Talk Radio Audiences.

You can use this information to send a more targeted message to stations that carry syndicated conservative or progressive talk shows. Or if you are buying radio time on a local station that carries the home baseball team or on a local outlet of ESPN radio, you may choose a sports-related theme or ambassador to advocate for your cause or candidate. Your media plan should include ads on radio stations with broad audiences in ethnic communities. Know the message environment into which you are sending ads or audio releases, or are seeking live airtime, so your media plan and budget will have maximum impact.

Radio ads are much cheaper than television ads, so you can buy large numbers of ads and dominate the airwaves for days at a time. These types of saturation buys are effective at motivating people to support your candidate or cause. Consider buying spots around a radio station's traffic and weather reports, since listeners tend to tune in for them at designated times every hour. It's even better if your message somehow relates to traffic (e.g., public transport and infrastructure issues) or weather (e.g., disaster preparedness, relief, or clean-up issues).

Audio releases. You can also purchase an MP3 player, computer software, or cloud computing services for recording public service announcements, commentary on issues, or reactions to a major news event. You can then e-mail the MP3 files to local radio stations as audio press releases. Although they are still canned, the releases do give you an opportunity to read your announcement or commentary in your own voice, and they help you connect with radio listeners.

Live airtime. Bill Press advises aspiring leaders to "listen to what's on the air" so they know the message environment, to call to inform the discussion with your message, and to book your most persuasive people as guests on talk radio. "Remember: producers have two to three hours to fill every day; they're always looking for strong, lively, provocative, well-informed experts on hot topics of the day."[6]

Blogs. Your main way to communicate with people online is through a blog you establish and through postings you make on community blogs that can distribute your message and ideas to online audiences, thank and update your supporters, and attract new people to your effort.

Every organization, candidate, or campaign should have a blog that records its activities and that calls others to service. An index or site map on your Web site should include your biography, mission statement, vision, ideas and values, service résumé, community maps and information, speeches and interviews, event news that is refreshed in real time, and streaming downloads. Invite volunteers to sign up online to join your effort or ask them to take your message or candidate to their neighbors, either by going door to door or by hosting a house meeting. Set up events in every corner of your community, and alert people by e-mail and through a centralized calendar as to when they can join you for house meetings, visibility activities, door knocking, and other events. Be sure to showcase photos from across the community to demonstrate the broad support and positive energy of your campaign.

Twitter users are now able to ask questions in advance or make comments in real time at debates, bringing voters closer to the action and the crowd-sourcing post-debate perceptions that used to be restricted to a handful of candidate representatives lined up in a room called Spin Alley.

Web advertising and analytics. Monitor popular blogs: review blogs that oppose your ideas for early warning signals of voter discontent or political attacks, and run banner ads on targeted blogs to drive people to your Web site. You will receive a report about how many people clicked on your ad and were directed to your Web site so you can assess your effectiveness.

Returning to our example of running for presidential delegate, you could run a Facebook ad targeting the pages of people who live within your community and limiting your ad buy to people who are "fans" of your candidate and your political party. That would quickly give you a universe of people who could be your own ambassadors. Your ad would send them to your official candidacy page or to an event where they could come and volunteer for you. Again, your theory is that these are mavens, connectors, and salespeople who are on Facebook in order to talk politics—so give them something to talk about: you.

By keeping current on events and posting your perspective on *Daily Kos*, the *Huffington Post*, or a local blog, you remain in the conversation. Before attending a public event or doing an interview, be sure you are up on the latest news. The morning paper is outdated the second it goes to press, but the paper's Web site is refreshed constantly.

Newspapers. Newspapers carry weight with their readers because there are journalists and fact-checkers who weigh in before a story that might be tweeted as gossip actually makes it past the filters to permanent ink. The Newspaper Association of America Web site (www.naa.org) indicates that three of four voters are regular newspaper readers and that one of two undecided voters look to newspapers in making up their minds about how to vote on election days.[7] Thus, newspapers are perfect for making serious arguments on an issue—promoting your vision (or taking apart the opposition) point by point. In addition, small community newspapers can sometimes be useful in reaching people interested in local news.

Opinion makers, reporters, politicians, community leaders, and large campaign contributors tend to be regular newspaper readers. A good newspaper ad or newspaper Web ad can create a buzz in these small circles. That buzz, in turn, can help create more positive media coverage and can motivate supporters to do more. Start with your local paper. Many newspapers have sections that differentiate by geographical zones. A balanced media mix must include online ads, in-paper ads, newspaper packaging inserts, or ads on the plastic delivery bags themselves that allow you to target your message to the zip codes of certain paper routes.

Community weeklies. Community weeklies and alternative media venues are often the most successful for emerging leaders because these papers sit in the barbershop and coffee house all week. The majority of emerging leaders and potential campaign workers will likely not get television coverage, and not everyone watches the nightly news or picks up the local daily paper.

The weeklies have their own special publication schedules. Many print midweek, so you must research deadlines. They are free, local to neighborhoods, and often read cover to cover.

Get your campaign events featured in community publications: church bulletins, senior center bulletins, and newsletters published by neighborhood groups. Many will welcome your additions. Remember, when it comes to bridging the digital divide, many older people and poorer people are not online, so you must reach them where they do receive information.

Billboards. Depending on their size and location, billboards can be effective for challengers or organizations with little or no name recognition. Candidates may giggle over buying the billboard across from their opponent's campaign office, but should do so only if the campaign has money to spare.

Direct mail. Direct mail is the medium most organizations and campaigns use to get their messages out. You can target direct mail at a particular audience more effectively than with any other medium. Voters are accustomed to receiving information in the mail, so they naturally pay attention to your message. Mail also allows you to send a specific message to a group of voters who care most about that issue. Use your resources— Community Inventory, micro-targeting, and local wisdom—to target people who are receptive to your message.

In 2010, Michael Rubio, a candidate for State Senate in California's Central Valley, sent mail to decline-to-state voters (not just Democrats). Despite a tough environment for Democrats, he cruised to victory because he built coalitions beyond his political party and added a positive personal touch.

Positive personal messages are always best because the mountains of mail that pile up on election eve and the pay-to-play slate cards have grown to annoy voters. Check the statistics and the feedback carefully before spending your money on mailings people may toss, resent, or both.

Telephones. With smart phones, digital recording, and high-speed communications, the telephone itself has become a medium. In 2009, 141 million landlines were in use combined with 286 million mobile cell phones and 245 million Internet users.[8] According to an August 2011 Pew survey, 29 percent of American households used cell phones and no landlines.[9]

Offer downloadable answering messages that supporters can customize and upload to their outgoing voice mail, and provide your campaign jingle—if you have one—as a downloadable ringtone.

Phone banks. As noted in chapter 5, phone banks can allow you to reach people in their homes, get their opinions on your issue or campaign, and encourage them to vote for your cause. Phones are a great vehicle for getting people to attend a house meeting or community activity, or for getting them out to vote, because you can contact them on Election Day. In low-turnout elections, this type of concerted effort can make a big difference.

Texting. Most new-media vendors enable you to send alerts inexpensively to inform people of upcoming events and urging them to RSVP to events or to support a cause or candidate. With a simple *Reply*, people can add to a computer-generated petition to a politician on an issue. After an action has been completed, a follow-up text can express thanks and share results. Again, read the Federal Trade Commission's CAN-SPAM Act very carefully. Get friends to text, message, or call their peers to encourage sign-ups.

Mix your media. The new media revolution is here. Campaigns must use all the tools available—Facebook to schedule events, Google Plus and banner ads to publicize them, Twitter to coordinate them, and YouTube to record them—so you must be versatile in all these venues. As you choose the elements of your media mix, consider how people in your community receive their information. That will drive your strategy. There is no template—only the needs that you research in your constituency. My personal preference is to use new media over network television and peer-to-peer over one-to-many.

If you are not Web savvy but your community is, you will need a good tutorial, so don't be shy in asking for help. At a 2011 Civil Society boot camp in Budapest, Hungary, I asked the group of NGO representatives and volunteers who used which type of media. Turned out the homeless advocates at Housing for All had an Internet radio capacity that the multi-national multi-million-dollar Habitat for Humanity did not. (They agreed to help train each other.)

Whichever mix you choose, remember that in each instance

you should consider your presentation with the essential public speaking advice: know your audience, connect with people, and talk to them the way they talk to one another.

WORK WITH THE MEDIA

Interacting with the media is essential to communicating with people. Follow the four rules of thumb: research the outlet (if not the journalist); respect media deadlines; present your message, not a script; and do not lie.

Do the research. As we saw in the previous section, it's crucial to research the media outlet and, if possible, whoever is covering you.

Respect media deadlines. A journalist's job is to get the news out, and your job is to get your message across. You must both do your jobs within certain time constraints. For television, everyone from the fact-checker to the anchorperson operates within the daily news cycle. This cycle starts in the morning and runs all day, until the final reporter files a story and the last television newscast ends. Be ready to amplify it during the day.

Understand the news cycle and dominate the news of the day. The news sites post stories at 4 a.m.; their editors and journalists go on cable at 7, 8, or 9 a.m. to drive the story. Then most shows pick up the stories and reactions thereto and run them for the day. So if you are trying to drive a conversation, you need to place your story online in the wee hours of a weekday morning and reinforce it. As a corollary, regardless of what you thought you wanted to discuss, once a news site is occupied with a big story, your message may get lost if you are not tying in your message with the theme of the day. Thus, any news or charge worth responding to should be responded to in the same news cycle as when it was made. Online journalists and new-media bloggers have even tighter deadlines, so be aware that respecting journalists' time is essential to a good working relationship.

Make your own media. Press conferences are your opportu-

★ ★ ★ ★ ★ ★ ★ ★ ★ ★ ★ ★

THE NEW NEWS CYCLE
by POLITICO Arena Senior Editor David Mark

POLITICO's Arena is a unique opinion/debate/discussion Web site focusing on the hot political issues of the moment. Arena editors maintain a list of about 300 "players" who receive each question and reach out extensively to members of Congress, celebrities, think-tank scholars and academics.

Like all of POLITICO, working in real time means there really are no news cycles or deadlines. When news breaks, Arena editors quickly send out questions, and answers usually begin pouring in within minutes. And while speed is key to Arena's success, old-fashioned journalistic values like accuracy and thoroughness reign supreme. These standards were tested January 8, 2011, after the tragic shooting of Arizona congresswoman Gabrielle Giffords, which she miraculously survived but which left several others dead.

Tucson was chaotic just after the shootings, with varied reports. I was tempted and felt it my responsibility to send out a question on the tragedy. But I knew from experience that would be a bad idea. I had been in the Capitol building on September 11, 2001, ▶

nity to advance your message and to make your own media. You will be generating news reports and campaign reports. You cannot count on the media to tell your story. You may be eclipsed by other events or by bias in coverage, so you must be sure to make your own media and release it to your supporters.

Be sure your communications team prepares well for press events and conferences. Prepare the visual and written portion of the event so the public knows exactly why this event fits in with your larger message. *Always* sweat the small stuff no matter who you are.

In July of 2011 the White House welcomed the World Series

> ▶ as a reporter for *Congressional Quarterly* and learned then that in
> crisis situations facts are quickly distorted and misinformation can
> spread quickly. Until the facts on the ground in Tucson were known,
> it would have been irresponsible to send a question. Hours later,
> once victims had been accounted for, I sent a cautiously worded
> question about whether various political players would try to use
> the episode to push their agendas.
>
> At other times finding appropriate questions amid high-profile
> stories is much easier, such as on a Sunday night in late April 2011,
> when the White House announced that President Obama would be
> speaking sometime after 10 p.m. The timing was unusual, to say
> the least. The White House news conference kept getting delayed—
> because as we found out later, President Obama was calling interna-
> tional allies. Then word began leaking through Twitter that al Qaeda
> leader Osama bin Laden, the mastermind of the 9-11 attacks,
> had been killed. As soon as POLITICO and the television networks
> confirmed the news, I sent out a question asking how the historic
> event would affect the war on terror. Several top-notch foreign policy
> analysts gave their views in Arena, in addition to important political
> voices on how the Obama administration's success in hunting down
> bin Laden might affect the president's 2012 election prospects.

champions—the San Francisco Giants. President Obama met the players, saluted the fans, and prepared to receive the team jersey. Always a step ahead, the president said, "OK, are we ready to move the podium?" when it was time for the team jersey photo. I turned to my mom and said, "He's the president and he's still his own advance man." If no detail is too small for the leader of the free world, it's not too small for the rest of us!

Present your message, not a script. The more automatic your answers, the more people will tune you out or try to trip you up. Either way, you will have lost an opportunity to express your passion for your call to service. Reporters will be looking for your personality, your response to pressure, and evidence of your work for people. Political reporters are particularly attuned to the question "Do you want to do something or do you want to be something?" because they continuously cover people who grow attached to the ego and fame associated with power. They can sniff out hypocrisy pretty quickly.

Phil Matier and Andy Ross write the eponymous column in the *San Francisco Chronicle* covering local and state politics. They advise that you should not run for office until you can identify "the comma behind your name"—that is, what you have done for people.[10] Just announcing that you have money and values and vision without presenting a track record will automatically place you at a disadvantage. If you are already in public service, be prepared to read your salary in the paper and to be able to justify it. "Public salaries and benefits are among our most-read and shared items," reveals Ross.[11]

Candidates, public employees, nonprofit staffers—everyone seeking or receiving taxpayer money must be prepared to communicate a reason for serving that is larger than themselves and justifies public confidence in them.

Do not lie. Here's a final rule. Know that at some point in every campaign, the "oh no" call is going to come from the media. It may be something you anticipate, like a past mistake you have already shared with your campaign leadership team, something you may have gotten an early warning about from your phone banking, or something you never saw coming.

In any event, the phone is ringing. "Face it and tell it," advise Matier and Ross. "Meet the question head-on, don't overspin, and don't be afraid to be right." If you need time, say so. Take time to consult with your kitchen cabinet. But you cannot put off the inevitable. You must respect the deadline, return the call, and *do not lie*.[12]

The reporter is judging you as a human being: Are you a good

★ ★ ★ ★ ★ ★ ★ ★ ★ ★ ★ ★

PRESS CONFERENCE CHECKLIST

★ Choose a location to fit your message. If you are talking about homelessness, go stand in front of a homeless shelter. Visit the site before calling the press conference.

★ Visit the site at the same time of day you will hold the press conference to be sure there is nothing to distract from your story.

★ Make visual content TV friendly. To compete with wars, fires, and floods, you need outstanding visuals. Time the event well. Avoid press conferences on Sunday or after 3 p.m.

★ Work out the speaking order in advance to eliminate awkward confusion in front of the microphone.

★ Call reporters a day in advance and give them a hint about what you are doing the next day. They will appreciate the notice.

★ Make a second round of pitch calls on the morning of the event. Check with the stations to find out which ones are sending cameras.

★ Practice answering tough questions that may come up.

★ Have something for reporters to hang microphones on if you don't have a podium.

★ *Always* sweat the small stuff.

★ Follow up with reporters after your event is over.

★ Post you own media from the event.

person who has made a mistake as humans do and will come clean, apologize, and move on, or are you someone who is going to lie? "This is the worst time for a reporter to dislike you," cautions Brad Martin.[13]

PREPARE FOR DEBATES

As you assert leadership in a public service effort, you may represent your cause or candidate in a debate. Debates are the rare venues in a campaign in which the outcome is up for grabs. Political debates have gone from freewheeling policy discussions in the last century to carefully scripted twenty-first-century television events. Thus, Americans took note when Bill Clinton left his podium at a 1992 debate and walked out in front of the audience to speak with the guests more closely. The very compactness of debates leaves room for that type of symbolic gesture.[14] On the other hand, when Mitt Romney laid a hand on Rick Perry during a 2011 CNN Republican presidential debate, many agreed that he had lost his cool and signaled a personal animosity that undermined the statesmanlike aura he was cultivating.[15] The lesson: get close to the audience but not your opponent.

When negotiating a debate format, think of how best to convey your message. If you are negotiating on behalf of a candidate for office, consider her habits. If she is comfortable with crowds, push for a town hall meeting format. If she is shorter than the others in the forum, press for a seated round table discussion. If she is the most knowledgeable on the issues, you may refuse to allow notes in the debate. Negotiate the smallest detail in favor of getting your message across.

Many people spend hours in debate preparation, simulating as much as possible the setting of the actual debate and using friends or volunteers to play the moderator and the opposition. This aggressive preparation always improves your performance, so if you are the one in the spotlight, overcome any resistance to practice, and discipline yourself to prepare. Now that debates are being broadcast and Webcast, with questions posed by viewers and online contributors, surf the Web in advance and prepare yourself for the curveball question.

Once the debate has started, respond to each question, enlarge the issue in your response, and then take the answer back to your message. If you are asked a divisive question, George Lakoff advises you to say so. "Be ready for questions presupposing your opponent's frames," he warns. "Rather than answer a question such as 'When did you stop beating your wife?' call it out: 'That question is designed to be divisive.' Then, go on to make your point."[16]

As with all media appearances, know your competitors, the moderator, and the audience. Go back to your message box where you researched your opponent—*What They Say about Them* and *What They Say about You*. Watch videos of the moderator in other forums to get a feel for her style and topics. Come prepared to make some news—either about yourself or the opposition. Then hammer away at your message throughout the debate. Everyone on stage is there to make news at someone else's expense, so be ready for an attack, and keep on message. Stay on message even during breaks. Remember: the microphone is always on. Follow up with a press statement underlining your message.

ENCOURAGE YOUR SUPPORTERS
TO INTERACT WITH THE MEDIA

You can serve your cause by putting forth your views on local media outlets and responding to misinformation that advances a biased story line. Here are some simple actions you and your supporters can take.

Your Web site should list media outlets, e-mail addresses, fax and phone numbers so that your supporters can communicate your message and monitor media coverage of your efforts. Display action alerts (urging supporters to speak out) and success stories (the results of any letters published or calls aired on your blog).

Write a letter to the editor. Letters to the editor are opinion pieces, so make sure your first sentence states your point of view. Make your letter short (two hundred words or fewer) and to the point. Newspapers often specify what information they need in order to publish a letter, so be sure your letter includes that information. Newspapers typically publish letters with the author's name and hometown (for example: "Jane Doe, Chicago"), so make sure whatever you say in your letter is something you would feel comfortable saying aloud in a room full of your friends and neighbors.

Call in to a radio show. "Callers drive talk radio," says Bill Press. He advises campaigns to "use talk radio to get the facts straight, reinforce your message, and let the community know what's going on and how to get involved."[17]

If you are the caller, remember Will Durst's advice and listen to a show before you call in to get a feel for what the hosts cover and the tone of their show. Call in to a show as early in the time slot as you can. Most radio shows have far more callers than can be accommodated on the air.

Write down your question or comment ahead of time so that if you do go on the air, you are prepared. Before you go on the air, you will briefly talk with a screener who helps the radio host select calls that will be appropriate and entertaining. The screener will ask your name, location, phone number, and the topic of your call.

Make sure the topic of your call is clear and concise. Keep it short and be polite. Also be in the moment—if you are interrupted before you can complete your point or question, kindly but firmly say, "Please let me finish my point." Stay calm—regardless of how the host responds to your point or question.

Monitor media bias. David Brock, who leads the watchdog organization Media Matters of America, enumerates elements of bias to look out for: distortions, errors, and misstatements; unbalanced coverage; misleading arguments; uncritical reporting; lack of coverage; repeating partisan talking points; and, extreme commentary. Although Media Matters' mission is to combat conservative misinformation, the following tools and tactics recommended by Brock may be used by anyone.[18]

Send a specific critique. Be polite. Keep it short. Be specific. The person who reads your e-mail should come away with a clear understanding of your request. Personalize your e-mail—but don't get personal. Each e-mail should be directed to one individual or media outlet and should refer to the coverage (or lack thereof) of that particular individual or outlet.

Contact advertisers. If a news outlet habitually presents misinformation, contact companies that financially support it or advertise on it and request they withdraw their support. Identify the companies whose advertisements appear most often, or visit the news outlet's Web site to determine who provides financial support. ColorofChange.org and Change.org are two grassroots petition Web sites that enable this crowd-sourced advocacy.

Get active locally. If a particular news reporter, radio host, or television personality in your community presents misinformation or fails to balance political views, draw attention to any misrepresentation of the truth. Search for local or state blogs that critique the media. They could be excellent sources for information or great potential allies.[19]

FOLLOW-UPS AND THANK-YOUS

With every communication, ask for support (membership, dollars, and votes), direct people back to your Web site, and thank them for their consideration. Then follow up with results of their work. "People want feedback on the success of what they've done," says Kerry Kennedy. "If you send a thank-you letter, they're committed. There should never be a time when people aren't thanked and recognized for past achievement and asked to participate in the next. If they never hear from you, you've lost them."[20]

Announcing the results—members joined, precincts walked, house meetings held, signatures collected, money raised, hits on a vlog, or texts for a cause—and thank-yous renew your connection with people and help them see the power of their work. Even if you did not reach your stated goals, remind people that you challenged them to service and that their *actions were appreciated and meaningful*. Letting people know results is not only good manners but good organizing: it will keep people engaged and invested in your efforts. People who did not participate in one action may see the results of another and be inspired to act next time.

Longtime labor organizer Fred Ross Sr. used to remind his activists: "People will appreciate what they do for you far more than what you do for them."[21]

★ ★ ★

GET REAL: DRAFT A COMMUNICATIONS PLAN WITH A BALANCED MEDIA MIX

The campaign manager and communications director should work out a media plan that will bring news to people the way they prefer to receive it, and talk to people the way they talk to one another.

Develop the plan through dialogue with the candidate or nonprofit leader and walk the communications team through the thinking behind the plan and its implementation, soliciting advice and expertise.

Present the plan to the campaign's leadership teams, since many of your team members have contacts with various members of the press or serve as bloggers or spokespeople in their own scope of service.

List media outlets. Find all that cover your community; include their Web sites, contact information, advertising options and rates, and timing of your proposed ads.

Outlets	Contact	Ad Options	Rates	Timing
Broadcast television				
Local cable				
Radio				
Blogs				
Newspapers				
Community weeklies				
Billboards				

Organize your messaging. List the activities that you will undertake to connect with people.

Activity	Message Topic	Budget	Timing
Mail			
Phone banks			
Texting			
Free "earned" media events			
Viral marketing			

Monitor the media. For each item, list media outlets and contact information; blog the results.

★ Action alerts (urging supporters to speak out)

★ Success stories (post results of any letters published or calls aired on blog)

SEVEN

★ ★ ★

Mobilize to Win

Whoever owns the ground wins the election.

HOUSE DEMOCRATIC LEADER NANCY PELOSI

Public service takes people. A passionate, engaged volunteer workforce can make your offices or campaign headquarters hum with excitement. That energy attracts people who want to join others who share their values, to promote a particular candidate or cause, or to gain recognition and respect in the community.

Whether you are running for president of the PTA or the United States, the team with the best volunteer operation will bring out the most voters on Election Day.

RECRUIT YOUR VOLUNTEER CORPS

Understand why people volunteer. People volunteer on campaigns for a number of reasons: to be part of a network of people who share their values, to promote a particular candidate or cause, or to gain recognition and respect in the community. Nearly all share the goal of making the future better.

Chris Finnie, a longtime Democracy for America (DFA) volunteer, expressed it this way: "After a Meetup, a woman stopped and asked me why I spent all the time and money I do on political activism. I told her I have a grown son. She said she did too. So I asked her if, when she had children, she didn't feel that she had given them a gift—a gift of life. She said yes. I then asked her if this was what she had in mind. She said no. I said me

189

either, and that's why I do what I do—so I can leave my son the sort of world I promised him."[1]

That was in 2007; now, four years later, we hear this same sentiment expressed by many people at the Occupy protests: the American Dream is slipping out of reach and only transformative change can get it back. Deep concern about the direction of the country can turn "slactivists" who merely sign e-mail petitions into activists marching in the streets. Volunteer coordinators must address those concerns and give people meaningful work.

Once your campaign has engaged volunteers, the most effective messengers are often the first-name friends and allies you knew before you got to politics. Congressmen Mike Honda and Tim Walz both found this to be true when they attracted former students and parents to their campaigns.

Mike Honda, a former teacher and principal from San Jose, California, was running for Congress in 2000 when his opponent's supporters put out a piece called "Honda's Criminal Record." In fact, Honda's only brush with the law was as an infant, when he and his Japanese American parents were placed in a World War II internment camp. Honda engaged former students and their parents to counter the attack via phone banks. One woman who was contacted said she'd heard about Honda's criminal record but was so glad that he had turned his life around that she'd vote for him.

Tim Walz, a former high school teacher and longtime Minnesota National Guardsman, earned the support of students he had taught and coached as well as of those with whom he had served in the reserves. When his opponent accused him of not understanding the military, Walz taped an ad on the football field pointing out that (in 2006) 3,000 troops had been killed in Iraq—about the number it took to fill the bleachers—some of whom he had seen dressed for football and dressed for war. Walz's powerful personal message was amplified by his former students, who validated his views on education and the war, and reinforced his good character.

Draw from people who have worked with you. To activate your networks, start as Honda and Walz did, by contacting and involving your friends and colleagues or those of your candidate. Look for a leader who can keep track of other volunteers and start scheduling regular volunteer activities. Build on your existing base. Ask your volunteers to host house meetings to bring their own friends into contact with the campaign. Invite whoever attends the first meeting to bring five friends to the next meeting. Then request the same at the next meeting. Soon, you will have a core group of hundreds of supporters.

Draw from organizations. Approach existing organizations that support your cause or candidate. Ask them to send people over to help with a specific project—knocking on doors or putting together a mailing. These people can help find other members of their organization who will get involved in your campaign.

If you are working with a political campaign, ask everyone on your team to carry volunteer sign-up cards at all times. Team members should ask everyone who expresses interest in volunteering to fill out a card and then call to involve them.

Reach out to young people. Empower and involve them at all levels of your public service effort. Arab American Institute founder James Zogby says: "It's like *Field of Dreams*—'If you build it, they will come.'" Zogby has issued calls for service in activities including voter registration, volunteering at events, participation in community cleanup days, and internships in Washington, D.C. "Young people want to serve. All you need to do is ask them and provide them with the opportunity."[2]

RETAINING YOUR VOLUNTEERS

When volunteers enter a vibrant campaign headquarters, your volunteer corps coordinator should greet them, give them a little tour to explain the activity, and then sit to talk about their call to service and reason for volunteering. The volunteer coordinator should match volunteers' skills and networks to the needs

★ ★ ★ CALL TO SERVICE ★ ★ ★

JAMES ZOGBY

James Zogby, executive director of the Arab American Institute, traces his call to service to the strong influence of his mother, who urged her children to get involved in community affairs. He recalls: "After receiving the benefit of a Jesuit education, I was challenged by my mother's injunction into civil rights and peace work. Later in my life, I took a long, hard look at the needs of my community, especially the most recent immigrants, and saw that as a challenge to service. My work in founding civic education projects to organize Arab Americans to vote and become involved in U.S. politics are but extensions of the early influences that motivated me toward service. Nothing gives me more pride today than to see immigrants become citizens and register to vote for the first time, and to see their children involved in our many internship programs, working in politics, civil rights, government institutions, and other forms of community service."

Now, ten years after 9/11, Zogby's Arab American Institute is still active in calling young people to serve and to counter the anti-Arab, anti-Muslim scapegoating still far too prevalent in American politics.

Source: James Zogby, e-mail, May 2007; James Zogby, conversation, September 10, 2011, Chicago, Illinois.

of the campaign and should train these new ambassadors with campaign protocols. Make sure volunteers clearly understand the tasks they perform, the issues they discuss, and how their efforts fit into the big picture and campaign plan.

If you are working with new volunteers, take ten or fifteen minutes to talk with them to make sure they are confident in what they are doing. See which of the 3Ps they are good at—people, paper, or physical skills—and match their abilities to tasks.

Pair them up with campaign staff or experienced volunteers to make a few calls or knock on a few doors together before you put them out on their own. Offer transportation if necessary. If people stay at the office late, offer to coordinate carpools for rides home. Give volunteers opportunities to meet other volunteers and campaign staff. Drop by the campaign office during the phone bank or precinct walk and thank volunteers for their time.

Give volunteers meaningful work and meaningful feedback. People who take time out of their own lives to help with the campaign expect to work when they arrive. Always make sure that you have a stack of work for volunteers to do. If someone shows up ready to knock on doors, get that person some materials and get them out into the community. Receive them when they return and find out how things went. A snack, a feedback form, and a brief chat will make them feel appreciated and give you valuable feedback. If volunteers feel that you do not need them, they will not come back, but if they believe that there is always important work to do, they will start showing up regularly.

Set and keep schedules, including regular training. Volunteer coordinators should set regular schedules for volunteers. This allows the campaign to schedule work to fulfill the service mission and tasks. Also, volunteers will come to think of the campaign as a regular part of their week. For example, the 1987 Nancy Pelosi for Congress Campaign gave volunteers a simple Campaign Calendar so that they could see how their work on the phone bank team or Ironing Board Brigade fit into the larger get-out-the-vote goals.

Feed your volunteers. An army marches on its stomach. The same is true for your volunteer army. Alec Bash and the Democracy Action network in San Francisco set up popular phone banks with coffee and bagels. The volunteer appreciation parties were sources of great food, lively conversation, and, of course, more recruitment.[3]

— CAMPAIGN CALENDAR —

MONDAY	TUESDAY	WEDNESDAY	THURSDAY	FRIDAY	SATURDAY	SUNDAY
A·P·R·I·L 27	28	29	30	1	2 MGT. OFF RALLY	3 IRONING BOARD BRIGADE
4	5 — PRECINCT LEADERS GET 3600 VOTES · BY MAIL / IRONING BOARD BRIGADES GETS 7400 VOTES · BY MAIL / PHONE BANK GETS 9000 VOTES · BY MAIL	6	7	**M·A·Y** **PHASE I** 8 PLANNING SESSION FOR NEIGHBORHOOD MEETINGS	9 IRONING BOARD BRIGADE	10 IRONING BOARD BRIGADE
11	12	13	14 PLANNING SESSION FOR NEIGHBORHOOD MEETINGS	15	16 IRONING BOARD BRIGADE	17 IRONING BOARD BRIGADE
18	19	20	21	22	23 IRONING BOARD BRIGADE	24 IRONING BOARD BRIGADE
25 LAST DAY TO TURN IN VOTE BY MAIL APP!	26	27	28 **G**	29 **O**	30 **T**	31 **V**
J·U·N·E 1	2 **PHASE II** ★ ELECTION DAY!					

Thank your volunteers. Keep your regular volunteers updated on the campaign, and let them know their contribution is making a difference. For example, "Thanks to your efforts on the phones last week, we've identified three hundred new supporters. We're right on track to reach our goals." Thom O'Shaughnessy, who was active with Veterans for Kerry in 2004 and now serves with the Los Angeles–area SoCal Grassroots network, says, "Volunteer recognition is vital." In 2006, the SoCal Grassroots network made campaign sun visors for people who walked three times and personalized sweatshirts for "Team Ann Richards," the cadre of people who walked weekend after weekend throughout the fall, dedicating their service to the late Texas governor. "These are some of my most treasured campaign items that I have received over all my years of field work," he says.[4]

Recognize volunteers officially. Thank-you letters, walls of fame, voter contact charts, and other forms of public recognition in your headquarters and on your Web site let volunteers know how much you value them. To use California Governor Jerry Brown's word, "tangibilitize" the volunteer experience: give them official recognition, research assignments that yield writing samples for a résumé, and certificates of appreciation.

Avoid—and do not condone—behavior that could lead to embarrassment. You never want to send your candidate on television to explain that your campaign was indeed responsible for some embarrassing act. The opposition is working hard enough to cause you problems, so there is no reason to cause your own. Beware of engaging in illegal or provocative behavior. Many a campaign has been forced to apologize when people were arrested for stealing or defacing signs. Internally, campaigns should offer basic training on anti-bullying and anti-harassment laws, and should post personnel procedures. As mentioned in chapter 2, campaign fraternization or transgressions can unfortunately become everyone's problem.

Track your volunteers. Maintain an electronic, regularly updated database of everyone who has volunteered or expressed an interest in volunteering on your campaign. Back up your database on a CD or other portable storage medium. Whenever possible, choose one person (your volunteer coordinator) to invite volunteers back to the campaign.

WALK THOSE PRECINCTS

Best practices for making house calls. A few tips for volunteers before you go knocking on doors.

First, think locally: when you go into a community, remember politics, sports, and revenge. Politics: if a popular elected official supports your candidate or cause, let voters know. Sports: some communities rally around athletic teams, and games are often played on weekends. Find out when the Big Game is, and don't walk or call then. In the special election of 2004 in Kentucky when Ben Chandler was elected to Congress, the Kentucky Wildcats football team was playing the Georgia Bulldogs the Saturday before the election. Precinct walkers for both Chandler and his opponent took a break between noon and 3 p.m., resuming work when the game ended. Revenge: if you are working for a ballot initiative that has been voted on before or canvassing for a candidate who lost to this opponent before, remember to show growth and not a grudge by keeping your approach oriented toward the future.

Second, act locally. What you say and do matters. Be polite and respect people. Your appearance matters, so dress comfortably and neatly. "The nose ring belongs on the bull in the field, not on the volunteer on the porch," advises national field strategist Donnie Fowler.[5] Be aware of the practices of different faiths in communities: Fridays, Saturdays, Sundays, and Wednesday nights are for worship, so voters could be headed to mosque, temple, church, or prayer night when you come knocking. Be ready to listen because voters may vent, especially if they are Independents, undecided, or people who are subjected to a lot of

★ ★ ★ ★ ★ ★ ★ ★ ★ ★ ★ ★ ★ ★ ★

MAKING HOUSE CALLS: BEST PRACTICES

Think Locally: Know the Customs of the Community

✓ Sports (When is the Big Game? Don't walk or call then!)

✓ Faith (Friday, Shabbes, or Sunday service; Wednesday prayer meeting)

✓ Weather (If the voter is in the storm cellar, you should be too!)

✓ Dress (Appearance matters to message)

Act Locally: What You Say and Do Matters

✓ Manners: R-E-S-P-E-C-T the voters

✓ Greeting: introduce yourself

✓ Listening: voters may vent!

✓ Talking: practice your script before calling or walking

✓ Thanking: carry the attitude of gratitude

Look Up: What's on the Air

✓ Know the Issues

✓ Know what ads each campaign is running (TV, radio, Internet)

✓ Listen to what people are saying about each campaign

Look Down: Read and Study

✓ Know your candidate

✓ Know the opposition

✓ Know local issues and events

Look All Around: What to Know or Whom to Call When

✓ You encounter reporters

✓ A voter needs to know where to vote

✓ A voter wants to vote early in person or by absentee ballot

✓ A voter talks about possible fraud or abuse of voting rights

Keep an Open Feedback Loop

✓ Volunteers: report back to HQ what is (or is not) working

✓ Campaigns: Put volunteer and voter comments in message box

✓ Remember: A positive attitude is everything!

ads. You are not there to argue with people in their homes but to persuade them through your enthusiasm and responsiveness to their feedback.

Third, know whom to call when a voter needs to know where to vote, wants to vote early in person or by absentee ballot, or talks about possible fraud or abuse of voting rights.

Fourth, keep an open feedback loop so that you can report back to headquarters what is or is not working. Use a message-box worksheet to set forth any new counterarguments coming from the volunteers or voters. If an attack mailer comes out and you can bring a copy back to the headquarters, the campaign can call in the kitchen cabinet to determine the best response.

Set up a canvassing operation. Go first to the areas where you are likely to find supporters. Pick the voters who are persuadable and who vote regularly. Pick the houses that have the largest raw numbers of voters in them. Then send your volunteers out to talk to them. The success of your canvassing program will depend on two things: how early you start and how organized you are. Once the basic research on your community is completed, you should know how many votes you will need to win. For each voter your canvassing program records as a supporter, you are one step closer to this goal.

Recruit precinct captains. Precinct captains are your most trusted and experienced volunteers who take responsibility for a precinct or geographical area. Precinct captains are well versed in how a canvassing operation works, the campaign's message, and the numerical goals in the particular precinct.

They are in charge of collecting walk sheets and reporting numbers from all the volunteers each time they walk and relaying them to the field manager. Good precinct captains will canvass and phone their precinct several times on their own and will recruit volunteers. In campaigns with limited staff, precinct captain systems provide invaluable levels of organization and

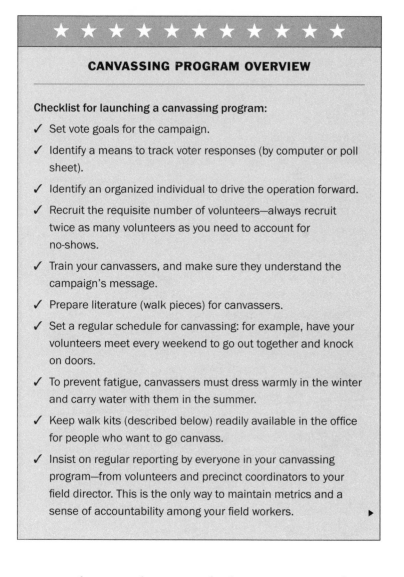

★ ★ ★ ★ ★ ★ ★ ★ ★ ★ ★ ★

CANVASSING PROGRAM OVERVIEW

Checklist for launching a canvassing program:

✓ Set vote goals for the campaign.

✓ Identify a means to track voter responses (by computer or poll sheet).

✓ Identify an organized individual to drive the operation forward.

✓ Recruit the requisite number of volunteers—always recruit twice as many volunteers as you need to account for no-shows.

✓ Train your canvassers, and make sure they understand the campaign's message.

✓ Prepare literature (walk pieces) for canvassers.

✓ Set a regular schedule for canvassing: for example, have your volunteers meet every weekend to go out together and knock on doors.

✓ To prevent fatigue, canvassers must dress warmly in the winter and carry water with them in the summer.

✓ Keep walk kits (described below) readily available in the office for people who want to go canvass.

✓ Insist on regular reporting by everyone in your canvassing program—from volunteers and precinct coordinators to your field director. This is the only way to maintain metrics and a sense of accountability among your field workers. ▶

ensure quality control in terms of volunteer training and accurate voter assessments.

To the extent possible, send the same volunteers to talk to the same voters. Then, on Election Day, send the volunteers to the polling places associated with the neighborhoods they have

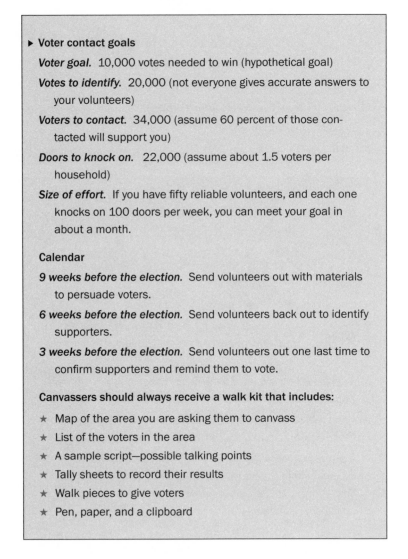

▶ **Voter contact goals**

Voter goal. 10,000 votes needed to win (hypothetical goal)

Votes to identify. 20,000 (not everyone gives accurate answers to your volunteers)

Voters to contact. 34,000 (assume 60 percent of those contacted will support you)

Doors to knock on. 22,000 (assume about 1.5 voters per household)

Size of effort. If you have fifty reliable volunteers, and each one knocks on 100 doors per week, you can meet your goal in about a month.

Calendar

9 weeks before the election. Send volunteers out with materials to persuade voters.

6 weeks before the election. Send volunteers back out to identify supporters.

3 weeks before the election. Send volunteers out one last time to confirm supporters and remind them to vote.

Canvassers should always receive a walk kit that includes:

★ Map of the area you are asking them to canvass

★ List of the voters in the area

★ A sample script—possible talking points

★ Tally sheets to record their results

★ Walk pieces to give voters

★ Pen, paper, and a clipboard

worked. The goal is make voters feel obligated to keep the promise they made to your canvasser to support your campaign.

Watch out for round numbers. Canvassers are talking to real people, so it is unusual for them to come back with exactly fifty supporters, thirty opposed, and ten undecided.

PLAN YOUR FIELD OPERATIONS

You must set a strategy to accomplish your goals that answers these questions:

★ How will we get the petition signatures needed to get on the ballot?

★ Who has custody of the most up-to-date voter file? How do we get it?

★ How many new voters do we need to register?

★ How will our canvassing program run?

★ How many volunteers will we need, and where will they come from?

★ How will we chase absentee and vote-by-mail voters?

★ How will our phone-banking program function?

★ How will our get-out-the-vote programs run?

Lay out your field plan. Design field work to fulfill three objectives: (1) identify the key demographic groups, geographic areas, or specific individuals who are most likely to support the campaign; (2) repetitively deliver the message to key groups, areas, and individuals to persuade them to support your effort; and (3) get those identified supporters out to vote on Election Day.

A successful field operation brings viability to a campaign and brings thousands of uninvolved people into the political process. A visible campaign becomes part of the message: when a campaign has grassroots support, it demonstrates that the cause has broad and deep consensus in the community or that the candidate is someone who is involved in the community and who cares about people.

Hire field organizers. Hire one field organizer at the start and use volunteers until you have the money and viability to hire more.

Open field offices. The job of a good field office is to hold literature, give volunteers a place to meet, and give workers a place to make phone calls. In the minds of many of your workers and volunteers, where you open field offices is a question of respect. Use house meeting hosts' homes for neighborhood headquarters sites so that you cover the entire community. Remember, people who cannot donate money may be able to donate garage space to store your campaign materials. Don't miss this opportunity.

Have field tools. You will want to have signs, literature, campaign fashion (hats, T-shirts, etc.), creative outreach (campaign song, video, map, poster, nail files, fans, etc.), and bilingual materials.

There are two times when campaign signs matter most— at the beginning and on Election Day. In the beginning, signs show strength. On Election Day, a few people may move in your direction if all their friends and neighbors appear to side with you. Focus on getting signs in homes and on lawns for that personal endorsement.

Budget your literature according to your ability to get it to voters. If you have three county chairpersons, each with twenty volunteers who are willing to work for ten hours each weekend, and there are three weekends remaining until the election, you have 1,800 hours of volunteer labor. If the average volunteer can deliver ten pieces of literature an hour to homes, then you should order 18,000 pieces of literature. Never order based on what you would like to get out—only on what you can really deliver.

PLAN YOUR VOTER CONTACT

Choose voter contact depending on your strategic objectives. If the initiative or candidate has a low level of name identification, the campaign must educate targeted voters about the candidate and the candidate's message before voter-identification efforts begin. If the campaign has financial assets, you can use early media and mailings to targeted voters. Campaigns with less money, but a large number of volunteers, can drop literature in targeted precincts or canvas door to door to raise name identification.

★ ★ ★ ★ ★ ★ ★ ★ ★ ★ ★

VOTER CONTACT

LOW-INTENSITY VOTER CONTACT

★ **Literature distribution.** "Lit drops" are the most basic form of campaigning. Place literature securely on the doors of houses in targeted areas. Do not put any campaign literature in mailboxes—doing so is illegal. Do not knock on doors or talk to voters during a lit drop. Lit drops are volunteer- and time-intensive but do not cost a lot of money.

★ **Leafleting.** Leafleting of public places like shopping centers or college campuses is less targeted than lit drops because you cannot tell (until you ask) who is taking your literature or where these voters live. Leafleting can build a crowd for an event.

★ **Visibility.** Visibility activities get the candidate's name out and raise the profile of the campaign. Examples include buttons, bumper stickers, lawn signs, billboards, and human sandwich boards.

HIGH-INTENSITY VOTER CONTACT

★ **Door to door.** Canvassing is one of the most traditional and effective forms of voter contact. An organized canvassing operation with well-trained volunteers yields excellent results ▶

Mix your voter contact techniques. Low-intensity activities are not individualized and not high impact. Low-intensity voter contact programs impart information about the candidate and can move voters but are not as persuasive as high-intensity programs, which are more individualized. High-intensity voter contact techniques often involve two-way communication. They give voters an opportunity to express their opinions about the candidate and the campaign.

▶   in persuading undecided voters. On the other hand, an un-
    organized operation with poorly trained volunteers can be a
    major drain of time and resources on a campaign and may
    lose votes.

★   **Phone banks.** Phone banks are one of the most commonly
    used forms of voter contact for voter identification, voter turn-
    out, volunteer recruitment, fund-raising, and crowd building.
    Be clear about the type of race you are in before you start your
    phone program. If you are simply trying to mobilize your core
    base of supporters to go out and vote, you probably need only
    one or two rounds of calls. If you are running a persuasion cam-
    paign, you will need to call more often. Most campaigns use
    "predictive dialers" that do the dialing for you, so you can be
    more efficient and reach only live people, not their voicemail.

★   **Candidate activity.** The most effective form of voter contact
    is the candidate asking someone face to face for a vote. The
    candidate's time is one of the most valuable and scarcest
    resources of every campaign. All of the voter contact portion of
    the candidate's time should be oriented toward reaching the
    highest number of persuadable voters. Engaging your message
    box, Community Inventory, and volunteer resources, assign
    the candidate's time to house meetings, town meetings, main
    street tours, door knocking, community events, and rallies.

Identify voters' priorities. Organize staff or volunteers to talk
to voters and ask their candidate preferences and opinions on
specific issues. This high-intensity method of gathering information allows campaigns to contact voters in a persuasive manner. Say your phone bank operation polled voters on the issues
and the candidates they were likely to support in the election.
Many respondents will report themselves undecided on the election, but most will be willing to rate the issues. Such a program

allows you to contact those undecided voters by mail with the campaign's position on the issues they consider most important. Concentrate your high-intensity voter contact in areas of poor party performance, where you have to do the most persuasion to move voters.

Respond to feedback. Whatever your voter contact techniques are, all require response to feedback. Remember your open feedback loop: voters give information to your volunteers who give it to your campaign. There must be a venue for the candidate to hear what voters think of the candidacy and the message and to provide answers and feedback. Voters' concerns will range from micro issues, such as a particular bill, which a follow-up phone call can answer, to macro issues, such as a character attack slung by the opposition, which warrants a much more publicly broadcast response. Either way, voters will expect you to respond to them. Use your kitchen cabinet, house meeting hosts, finance council, and election protection team to find out what questions are out there and what responses are (or are not) resonating.

CONVENE A CAMPAIGN TEAM BOOT CAMP

Public service campaigns are marathons. They take months to build before the public tunes in. A marathon is 26.2 miles, but the public is tuning in at mile 24, just when you are getting tired. Set aside some time approximately seventy-five days before Election Day to convene a campaign boot camp to lock in a winner or adjust while you can.

With your team, perform the exercises from each of the chapters to assess, update, and take an honest measure of your campaign. Hope is not a strategy: base your final planning on what you actually have accomplished and build from there. Review the seven steps of the Boot Camp to lock in or adjust your tactics and take the Get Real exercise at the end of this chapter to plan ahead.

PLAN YOUR GET-OUT-THE-VOTE STRATEGY

Encourage early voting. In many communities, voter registrars allow people to vote up to thirty days before Election Day. This means that canvassing must include an early voting strategy. If you have a good voter file, you can identify people, get their addresses into the system, and send them an e-mail at the start of early voting. Shortly before the election, crosscheck the voter file against the list of voters who have already voted. If your targeted supporters are not recorded as voting, send them another e-mail the weekend before the election.

Promote vote-by-mail/absentee balloting. Votes cast by mail have a major impact on elections in many states. Check the rules of your state and plan accordingly.

A good vote-by-mail/absentee-ballot program requires your campaign to identify your supporters, target those with a weak voting history and those who have voted by mail in the past, and walk those voters through the process of casting their ballots by mail. This process generally means mailing and calling voters several times. Before launching a vote-by-mail program, you must have a reliable method to track the voters you have targeted.

Start with the voter file you purchased to prepare your Community Inventory. Then update your file with information from your Community Inventory, networks, publicly available data, and canvassing contacts. Get an updated list from the voter registrar to include people who have registered to vote since you began this process.

If your polling or other research indicates that your initiative or candidate has strong support among the most infrequent voters, you may choose to immediately target this group for your vote-by-mail program. Otherwise, you will probably start with canvassing and phone calls to identify supporters who do not frequently vote.

The key is to conduct a sustained conversation between the campaign and your target voters. This may mean mailing to the group several times and then following up with phone calls to make sure their ballots have actually been mailed. A final phone call should remind those who have not already returned their ballots to vote in person on Election Day. As with every other part of the campaign, your goal should be to walk the voters through the entire vote-by-mail process, so they know when to request a ballot, how to fill it out, when to mail it back, or where to drop it off. And check with the Department of Elections to see that it was received.

Study the different voting patterns among the absentee voters. Divide absentee voters into two categories and track them separately: (1) people who always get absentee ballots and always vote; (2) people who always get absentee ballots but do not always vote. Obviously, the second group needs a bigger push to send in their ballots. When ballots are mailed out to absentee voters (usually four weeks before the election), canvass to encourage people to send in their ballots. Later, in the final days before the election, canvass the people who have not voted and encourage them to mail their ballots or drop them off at their polling places.

Your goal should be to start Election Day with as many votes already in the bank as possible. A well-run vote-by-mail program can get your votes in early and inoculate your campaign against last-minute attacks.

RALLY THE ALL-STARS

The final days of a campaign sum up what the election is about. If you are running for office or volunteering on a campaign, bring your people together *now* and persuade voters to go to the polls. To get last-minute media attention and rally the troops, bring in the all-stars.

For candidates, the all-stars bring a final boost to campaign efforts. For volunteers, this is a reward for hard work and a

★ ★ ★ ★ ★ ★ ★ ★ ★ ★ ★ ★

GET-OUT-THE-VOTE SCHEDULE

ONE MONTH PRIOR TO ELECTION DAY

★ Canvassers identify enough voters to meet their vote goals.

★ Based on canvass results, choose target areas for the Election Day operation. (Put workers in strong areas where they can get the most supporters to the polls.)

★ Sign up two-thirds of the Election Day volunteers needed for your get-out-the-vote plan.

★ Choose a location for Election Day training and/or final rally.

★ Set the content of Election Day materials for captains, poll watchers, and workers.

★ Make a complete list of all polling places.

★ Place printing order for Election Day sample ballots and door-hangers.

★ Set the location of the victory party.

THREE WEEKS BEFORE ELECTION DAY

★ Organize Election Day volunteers by precinct.

★ Produce copies of Election Day training packet.

★ Canvassers speak to undecided voters and people voting with absentee ballots.

★ Identify sites where phone calls can be made during Election Day.

TWO WEEKS BEFORE ELECTION DAY

★ Sort Election Day materials in the campaign office by precinct.

★ Prepare voter lists for precinct captains and poll watchers.

★ Purchase polling place materials: supplies, tape, pens, etc. ▶

► ## TEN DAYS PRIOR TO ELECTION DAY

★ Train Election Day workers and volunteers.

★ Give precinct captains and poll watchers Election Day training kits to read.

★ Captains receive a list of supporters as well as signs, staplers, tape, and pens. They also get a list of volunteers assigned to them.

★ Give Election Day workers their precinct assignments.

TWO DAYS PRIOR TO ELECTION DAY

★ Captains and volunteers prepare for get-out-the-vote on Election Day.

★ Captains call the volunteers assigned to them to confirm and check who needs a ride.

ELECTION DAY

★ Poll watchers arrive at 5:30 a.m. and supervise the preparations to open the polls.

★ Volunteers place door-hangers at homes of voters, avoiding homes with dogs if possible—no need to wake the neighbors!

6 A.M.—POLLS OPEN

★ Poll watchers and passers are in place.

★ Poll watchers begin crossing off names, and passers begin handing out sample ballots.

★ Precinct captains phone in to headquarters and give status reports.

★ Captains buy coffee and doughnuts for their workers.

9 A.M.—CALLS BEGIN

★ Phone calls to supporters start from various locations and continue throughout the day. ►

10 A.M.—FIRST RUN

★ Poll watcher gives precinct captain the names of all identified voters who have not voted.

★ Precinct captain gives info to drivers, who visit supporters' homes and give election reminders.

★ Precinct captain calls the office to ensure everything is going smoothly and then buys breakfast for the volunteers.

★ Field director may give orders to move volunteers according to poll watcher results.

2 P.M. & 5 P.M.

★ Poll watcher gives precinct captain the names of all identified voters who have not voted.

★ Precinct captain gives cards to drivers, who visit supporters' homes and give election reminders.

★ Precinct captain calls the office.

★ Field director may give orders to move volunteers according to poll watcher results.

6 P.M.

★ Poll watcher gives precinct captain the names of all identified voters who have not voted. Precinct captain gives cards to drivers, who drive any remaining voters to the polls.

8 P.M.

★ Poll watcher and precinct captain remain until every voter in line has an opportunity to vote.

★ Volunteers clean up signs and other campaign literature around the polls.

9 P.M.—VICTORY PARTY

★ Poll watcher and precinct captain observe the ballot counting and let election protection team know of any difficulties.

Source: AFSCME P.E.O.P.L.E./New House PAC, *2006 Congressional Candidates Boot Camp Manual*.

motivator for the last push to the polls. For voters, it is an opportunity to see the individual campaign in a larger perspective.

Democrats' top draws aside from sitting politicians are former President Clinton, former Vice President Al Gore, and First Lady Michelle Obama; Republicans have been drawing former potential 2012 candidates like Mississippi's Haley Barbour and Wisconsin's Paul Ryan as well as various FOX News personalities.

Remember that if you bring in talent like musicians or comedians, they are viewed as political ambassadors for your campaign, so keep them on message.

THE HOME STRETCH:
DEMONSTRATE STAMINA AND LEADERSHIP

It is also the time to stay focused: at the end of a marathon, people are tired and are more likely to make mistakes or lose focus. Disciplined campaigns run like they are behind even when polls say they are ahead; they stay focused and use rapid response to counter late hits. As a candidate, campaign worker, or issue advocate, you will have to demonstrate stamina and leadership in the final pressure-filled days.

Stay focused in the final days. Candidates and volunteers often go without sleep or get nervous, and that's when a gaffe can derail the best of campaigns. In the recovery movement, they say that people are most likely to relapse when they are hungry, angry, lonely, or tired (HALT).

In that spirit, think HALT—and literally halt. If you are hungry, eat something. If you are angry, shrug off political attacks rather than taking them personally. If you are lonely (politically speaking), reach out to a broader audience and connect with people who are there to help the campaign come together. If you are tired, get some sleep. In the last few days, candidates may be asked trick questions, so be especially careful that *everyone* on the team—the candidate, volunteers, or issue advocates—has the presence of mind to HALT and display grace under pressure.

ELECTION DAY

To run a good Election Day operation, you need a Get-Out-the-Vote (GOTV) team consisting of an election protection team, field director, precinct captains, poll watchers, passers, drivers, phone callers, and office staff in place. These are their assignments.

Your GOTV Team

Election protection team. These legal observers should include attorneys specializing in election law to answer any questions coming in from the poll watchers or precinct captains. In the case of disputes, it helps to have an attorney available to send to a precinct if there is a problem. They can use cell phone and video cameras to record incidents and work with election incident clearinghouses. Donna Brazile counsels, "The election protection team's primary responsibility is to anticipate and address uninformed poll workers, new voting systems, purges of voter registration lists, voter suppression, misinformation, and intimidation tactics. The team's goal is to ensure the elections are being administrated in a fair and transparent manner. The more issues addressed in advance, the more access voters will have to the process."[6]

Field director. Your campaign must make adjustments throughout the day in response to information coming in from the field. This may mean shifting volunteers to areas when large numbers of your supporters are not showing up to vote.

Precinct captains. Precinct captains must be your generals who keep field operations in their precincts running smoothly, use resources judiciously, and notify headquarters immediately of any potential problems. Specific responsibilities of the precinct captain include making sure that all volunteers get to the poll-

MOBILIZE TO WIN   213

ing place on time, that the polls open and close on time, that all volunteers get breakfast, snack, and lunch, and that all identified voters get to the polls to vote. *Your precinct captains must be reliable.* Test them at various intervals throughout the campaign to identify who can perform and who cannot. Ask precinct captains to phone or text in their numbers to the office when the polls open, at 10 a.m., 2 p.m., 5 p.m., and after the polls close.

Poll watchers. This is the most important job inside the polling place on Election Day. Poll watchers track everyone who votes. You must have an accurate list of all supporters who have not voted so you can get these people to the polls. Because this is a tedious, all-day job, assign a morning and an afternoon poll watcher for each precinct. Poll watching is also a technical job, so your election protection team must train these people.

Passers. Assign a minimum of two people to each polling place. These people are responsible for visibility. They start their day by placing your signs around the polls one hour before they open. They finish by removing all campaign signs. During voting hours, they should station themselves outside the polling place to distribute your literature and sample ballots. Consult your state election law for any restrictions on passing out literature at or near the polling place.

Drivers. There are two functions for drivers. The first is to help walk precincts. As the California SoCal Grassroots and Take Back Red California networks did, adopt the term *strike team* from firefighting. Use a coordinated strike team of a driver and two or three walkers so as to blitz a precinct in a short time for maximum penetration. A team of travelers can be used most effectively if it includes one local volunteer who knows the territory. Drivers drop off the walkers at the top of the hill and then wait at the bottom to collect the walkers and continue on.

Drivers also pick up supporters who need a ride to the polls.

During the day, the poll watcher should supply the precinct captain with a list of names of nonvoting supporters at 10 a.m., 2 p.m., and 5 p.m. The captains pass along these lists to drivers, who visit each house on the list, remind the people to vote, and offer them a ride to the polling place.

Phone callers. Assign at least one person per precinct to remind all supporters to vote. The reminder calls can start as early as 8 a.m. and should continue throughout the day.

Office staff. Everyone should be in the field with only a skeleton staff at the headquarters to make sure that things are flowing smoothly and to patch holes where there are problems.

Protect the Vote

First, know your voters. Your election protection team must have the final list of your voters and be aware of voter ID laws or hot button issues. If your election authorities allow same-day registration, know the eligibility requirements.

Second, know your voting rights. The three most basic voting protections to remind voters of are these:

★ You have a right to view a sample ballot at the polling place before voting.

★ If you are in line before the published closing time, you are entitled to cast a ballot.

★ If you have problems, you are still entitled to cast a provisional ballot (although I recommend calling a voter helpline and a judge before casting a provisional ballot).

Third, know your ballot. With several races on the ballot at once, you will want voters to find your candidate or ballot initiative easily. If your candidate is running against a dozen people for city council and voters can pick up to three choices, let them know that in advance. If your community has ranked choice or instant runoff voting, be sure your supporters and poll watchers have explained the process to your voters. Finally, if you have paper ballots, be sure that people know to vote on the front and back sides of the ballot.

Fourth, know your voting systems. Your election protection team will have a list of the types of voting machines (paper ballots, punch cards, touch screens, optical scanners, etc.) used at each precinct. That way, your poll watchers know the types of equipment for casting and counting ballots, the challenges unique to particular systems, any research regarding possible tampering and computer malfunctions of the machinery—particularly with the touch screens—and whether there are sufficient protections for disabled voters so that, pursuant to federal law, they can vote independently.

Fifth, know your legal options. A smooth election protection operation allows poll watchers and hotlines to solve election problems before anyone casts provisional ballots. When your poll watchers identify problems, they should contact a member of your election protection team who can work on the problem— and even call a judge if necessary. Better to work out the challenge beforehand if possible, rather than adding a vote to the pile of provisional votes that may or may not ever be counted.

Sixth, document everything. In case of a recount or challenge, sworn affidavits and cell phone videos of the challenges make the evidence more tangible. In the end, your election records should demonstrate that your team took exquisite care to ensure that the laws were followed and that the votes were counted as cast.

The goal is to wake up after Election Day with no regrets. You have performed according to the highest ideals of your call to service, you have excelled at management, message, money, and mobilization, and you have done your best to make sure that everyone has voted and that all the votes were counted as cast.

★ ★ ★

GET REAL: BOOT CAMP CHECKLIST

As you head into the last seventy-five days of the campaign marathon, convene a campaign boot camp to lock in a winner or readjust as needed. Gather your team together and consider the following:

Identify your call to service

★ Does your campaign reflect your service mission?

★ Are you fulfilling the promises and commitments you made?

★ Did you commit the necessary time, energy, and resources?

★ If not, what would you change?

★ How is family life? Is everyone still on board?

★ Does the campaign reflect the vision, ideas, and values that inspire the call to service?

Define your message

★ Is your message getting out there?

★ How have allies and attacks affected people's perceptions of the campaign?

★ Anything you need to change here?

Know your community

★ Has the campaign visited every possible neighborhood and major event?

★ Do you have the coalitions built and can you engage networks of support?

★ Have you identified your winning number and can you reach that goal?

Build your leadership teams

★ Do you have the people in place to succeed?

★ Did you fully commit yourself and hire people who work well together?

★ How has the kitchen cabinet handled surprises and setbacks?

★ Are the house meeting hosts having events and building the volunteer corps?

★ Did people come through?

★ Did the money calls get made?

★ Are there people you can still pull in before the filing deadline to fund the last push?

★ Should you add more fund-raising at house meetings or during call time to get the funds needed to meet the budget?

★ What is your adjusted plan—according to what is real, not what you hoped to raise?

Connect with people

★ Have you reached the people where they live?

★ Any positive debate moments to broadcast or gaffes to overcome?

★ What is your online presence?

★ Who have been your best allies and ambassadors? Are they available in the final days to help?

Mobilize to win

★ Have you recruited a volunteer corps who will talk to strangers, walk precincts in the rain, and sleep on floors or open their homes?

★ Where can you conduct more house meetings?

★ What networks might you tap for additional support to achieve victory on Election Day?

After-Action Review

What do we do now?

ROBERT REDFORD, *THE CANDIDATE*

YOU WON! NOW WHAT?

You have answered the call to service. You exercised your right to vote or to peacefully assemble for a cause and you fulfilled your commitment to serve your campaign or cause. The race has ended, and the voters have chosen you. Now what? The marathon begins.

Six keys to enduring success: review your campaign, prepare for the transition, do the job, stay close to your people, keep your word, and pay it forward.

Review your campaign. Review the following in terms of quality, timeliness, and usefulness:

1. Personnel and networks
2. Process for defining, refining, repeating, and refreshing message, including campaign pledges, promises, and commitments made on the trail
3. Ambassadors and allies
4. Communications strategy and media plan
5. Criticisms raised by citizens, local media, and opponents (Note what the responses were at the time and in retrospect what they should have been.)
6. Plan for budgeting and raising money
7. Process for mobilization—recruiting, training, and retaining—of volunteers

Prepare your transition. Keep campaigning and governing separate. The people who helped you get elected are not necessarily the best people to serve in government, so be very careful
about automatically transferring personnel. People need policy
credentials and management skills before you assign them the
work of legislation and casework.

Do the job. Your community elected you to do something. Do it.
Throughout your campaign, you articulated the type of leadership that the job required, and you put yourself forward as the
leader who could do it best. That may mean conducting yourself
differently now. You are no longer a challenger or candidate;
you are the representative of your constituents. Represent them.

"People need to know that you will provide full representation to everyone, including those who openly acknowledge that
they did not vote for you," says Willie L. Brown Jr. He advises
incumbents: "Define and perform your job so well that *no one
but you can do it.* Whether you define the job as constituent
contacts and services, perfect voting attendance, or complete
knowledge of a particular subject, do your job in a unique and
excellent way."[1]

Stay close to your people. Remember, everything you do or don't
do, everything you say or don't say communicates to your community. Start your term in office with a listening tour. If your
ballot initiative passes, update the public—and your supporters
in particular—when the new law goes into effect or when its
benchmarks are reached. Maintain your feedback loops and your
community networks in person and online. People should see
the results of your work.

As Bay Area Democrats' cofounder Wade Randlett says,
"Winning the election is just the first day. Now you have to do
the thing you believe in. You need to have the people with you
to do the thing you said you would do. Campaigning is creating
that connection. If you lose that connection you did yourself a

disservice because you are not keeping the power to make the change you ran to make in the first place."[2]

Keep your word. When you launched your campaign, you committed to serve your community, and you promised to improve the future of your constituents. Keep your word. If you promised to forgo certain perks, forgo them. If you promised to show up at all the meetings, show up prepared. If you promised to post your schedule on your Web site, post it. If you promised to hold public meetings, hold them. Nothing un-elects people faster than breaking their word.

Pay it forward. Throughout your campaign, people gave to you. They gave you their time, their money, their talent, their vote. Give back. Mentor others. Somewhere in your community, future leaders already walk in your footsteps.

Notes

Chapter One

1. For example, see President Obama's weekly address to the nation, December 22, 2010. http://www.cbsnews.com/video/watch/?id=7176586n.

2. George F. Will, column, *Washington Post*, September 11, 2002; e-mail, May 17, 2007.

3. "Most Continue to Favor Gays Serving Openly in Military," Pew Forum on Religion & Public Life, November 29, 2010. http://pewresearch.org/pubs/1812/dont-ask-dont-tell-repeal-public-supports-gays-serve-openly-in-military.

4. Nancy Pelosi, Amy Hill Hearth, *Know Your Power: A Message to America's Daughters* (New York: Random House, 2008).

5. Lezlee Westine, interview, June 12, 2007.

6. Ibid.

7. Jennifer L. Lawless and Richard L. Fox, "Why Don't Women Run for Office?" Brown University Policy Report, January 2004.

8. Ellen Malcolm, interview, June 29, 2007; www.sheshouldrun.org.

9. Annete Tadeo, remarks to Florida Young Democrats Convention, Ft. Lauderdale, FL, June 11, 2011.

10. "Turning Point: The Changing Landscape for Women Candidates," Barbara Lee Family Foundation, Summer 2011.

11. Kerry Kennedy, interview, April 4, 2007.

12. "Don't Get Caught in a Bad Hotel," YouTube, http://trueslant.com/suefrause/2010/05/12/dont-get-caught-in-a-bad-hotel-lady-gaga-flashmob-at-the-westin-st-francis/.

13. Rhonda Bodfield, "Giffords to Vote for Health-care Reform, Says It's the 'Right Thing to Do,'" *Arizona Daily Star,* March 20, 2010. http://azstarnet.com/news/local/govt-and-politics/article _9dac2462-3497-11df-aa7c-001cc4c002e0.html?mode=story#ixzz1 WVMV5hs6.

14. "Video of Representative Giffords Discussing Violence," MSNBC, uploaded January 8, 2011. http://openchannel.msnbc.msn .com/_news/2011/01/08/5792846-video-of-interview-with-rep -giffords-discussing-violence.

15. Mary Hughes, interview, April 10, 2007; www.the2012project .us.

16. Jack Valenti, remarks to National Italian American Foundation, Washington, D.C., June 3, 2004.

17. Jeff Dyer, Hal Gergensen, and Clayton M. Christensen, *The Innovator's DNA* (Boston: Harvard Business Press, 2011).

18. Tim Roemer, "Winning Lessons in Red States for Blue Candidates," *Trail Mix,* May 23, 2006.

19. Bevan Dufty for Mayor, "Someplace New," YouTube, uploaded September 30, 2011. http://www.youtube.com/ watch?v=oT9CE0vYEEI&feature=youtube_gdata_player.

20. Jan Brown, e-mail, July 2007.

Chapter Two

1. Kirsten Gillibrand, speech, San Francisco, May 31, 2007. www .offthesidelines.org.

2. Jamal Simmons, interview, May 16, 2007.

3. Mary Hughes, interview, April 10, 2007.

4. "Dick Scaife: Republicans Wrong on Planned Parenthood" op-ed, *Pittsburgh Post-Gazette,* February 27, 2011. http://www .pittsburghlive.com/x/valleynewsdispatch/s_724838.html.

5. Mary Hughes, interview, April 10, 2007.

6. David Mark, e-mail, September 3, 2011.

7. Ibid.

8. David Mark, e-mail, November 2, 2011.

9. Dotty LeMieux, e-mail, May 18, 2007.

10. Carl Pope, interview, March 27, 2007.

11. Ibid.

12. Ibid.

13. Brad Martin, speech, May 26, 2007.

14. Frank Luntz, Web site: www.luntz.com/where_overview.html.

15. George Lakoff, interview, June 12, 2007.

16. California Democratic Party, "Stay Jerry, My Friends," YouTube, uploaded October 25, 2010. http://www.youtube.com/watch?v=LZHO0LEhQPk .

17. Andrew Levison, *Democratic Strategist*, October 21, 2011. http://www.democracycorps.com/strategy/2011/10/the-democratic -strategist-on-democracy-corps-innovative-polling/.

18. Maggie Linden, speech, DNC Western Caucus conference, August 13, 2011, Sacramento, CA. http://www.youtube.com/watch?v=KhN_fgwLz3E.

19. Dotty LeMieux, "Ten Common Mistakes Novice Candidates Make: Myths and Facts to Help the First Time Candidate Get Off to a Sound Start," *Campaigns and Elections*, June 2003.

20. Max Cleland, "Wireside Chat," *Trail Mix*, April 30, 2006.

21. Dr. Rachel Kleinfeld, e-mail, September 6, 2011.

22. Larry Margasak, "Foley Resigns from Congress over E-mails," *Associated Press*, September 30, 2006.

Chapter Three

1. Mary Hughes, interview, April 10, 2007.

2. Malcolm Gladwell, *The Tipping Point* (New York: Little Brown and Company, 2000).

3. Mary Madden and Kathryn Zickuhr, "65% of Online Adults Use Social Networking Sites," Pew Internet and American Life Project, August, 2011. http://www.pewinternet.org/Reports/2011/Social-Networking-Sites.aspx.

4. Markos Moulitsas, e-mail, June 25, 2007.

5. Gerald W. McEntee, interview, April 25, 2007.

6. Markos Moulitsas, e-mail, June 25, 2007.

7. Tim Tagaris, e-mail, June 2, 2007; "My ATM Pin Number or Fundraising On-line," *MyDD*, December 23, 2004. http://www.mydd.com/story/2004/12/23/114450/18.

8. Bruce Braley for Congress Web site: www.brucebraley.com.

9. Press Release, Democratic National Committee, "Debbie Wasserman Schultz Elected DNC Chair," May 4, 2011. http://www.democrats.org/news/blog/breaking_news_debbie_wasserman _schultz_elected_dnc_chair.

10. John F. Tierney, e-mail, June 7, 2007.

11. Mike Thompson, conference call, September 15, 2005.

12. Dotty LeMieux, e-mail, May 19, 2007; "The Ties That Bind: Successful Coalition Building for Referendum or Initiative Campaigns," *Campaigns & Elections*, August 2005.

13. Celinda Lake, interview, July 9, 2011.

14. Matt Singer, speech, DNC Western Caucus conference, Sacramento, CA, August 13, 2011. http://busproject.org/.

15. Celinda Lake, speech, DNC Western Caucus conference, Sacramento, CA, August 13, 2011.

16. Ronald Reagan, remarks at a reception for delegates to the State Republican Convention, New York City, June 17, 1982. www.reagan.utexas.edu/archives/speeches/1982/61782e.htm.

17. Brad Martin, "Best Practices for Primary Winners," *Trail Mix*, June 15, 2006.

18. Donnie Fowler, interview, May 16, 2007.

19. Ibid.

22. Alex Clemens, interview, April 11, 2007. www.SFUsual Suspects.com.

Chapter Four

1. Dotty LeMieux, e-mail, May 21, 2007; "Ten Common Mistakes Novice Candidates Make," *Campaigns & Elections*, June 2003.

2. George F. Will, column, *Washington Post*, March 15, 2007.

3. Willie L. Brown, Jr., interview, March 27, 2007.

4. Jim Gonzalez, e-mail, May 30, 2007.

5. Larry Scanlon, speech, DNC Western Caucus conference, San Francisco, CA, May 25, 2007.

6. Bill Clinton, speech, liveblogged by the author from John Lewis's front porch, Atlanta, GA, October 25, 2006.

7. Jamal Simmons, interview, May 16, 2007

8. Lezlee Westine, interview, June 12, 2007

9. Craig Newmark, interview, August 22, 2011.

10. Sophia Yan, "How Scott Brown's Social Media Juggernaut Won Massachusetts," Time, February 4, 2010.

11. Donna Brazile, e-mail, June 4, 2007.

12. Brennan Center for Justice, "Voting Law Changes in 2012," 2011. http://www.brennancenter.org/content/resource/voting_law_changes_in_2012.

13. DNC Voting Rights Institute, "The Real Cost of Photo I.D. Laws," 2011. www.democrats.org/the-real-cost-of-photo-id-laws?source=DSH.

14. Nick Wing, "GOP-Linked 'Latinos For Reform' Airs Nevada Ads Urging Hispanics Not To Vote," the *Huffington Post*, October 19, 2010. www.huffingtonpost.com/2010/10/19/latinos-for-reform-vote-nevada_n_767991.html.

15. Maria Teresa Kumar, *Voto Latino*. "Statement on the Don't Vote Campaign," October 20, 2010. www.votolatino.org/voting/ 2010/10/20/voto-latino-statement-on-the-dont-vote-campaign/.

16. Wade Henderson and Mark Perriello, op-ed in the *Progressive*, July 18, 2011; Figures sourced at http://smlr.rutgers.edu/fact -sheet-on-disability-and-voter-turnout-in-2010.

Chapter Five

1. Rachel Binah, e-mail, May 16, 2007.

2. Dotty LeMieux, e-mail, May 18, 2007.

3. Rachel Binah, e-mail, May 16, 2007.

4. Wade Randlett, interview, August 11, 2011.

5. Dino Grandoni, "Consultant Found Guilty of Stealing $1 Million from Bloombert," *Atlantic Wire*, October 21, 2011.

6. Tony Perry, "Durkee May Be Bernie Madoff of Campaign Treasurers," *Los Angeles Times*, September 12, 2011.

7. Brian Wolff, interview, June 21, 2007.

8. Chris Murphy, discussion, June 6, 2007.

Chapter Six

1. Will Durst, interview, April 10, 2007.

2. "George Allen Introduces Macaca," YouTube, August 15, 2006.

3. Andrea Dew Steele, interview, May 2007.

4. George Ray, speech, DNC Western Caucus conference, San Francisco, May 26, 2007.

5. Bill Press, e-mail, July 19, 2007.

6. Ibid.

7. Jack Brady, speech, DNC Western Caucus conference, May 25, 2007.

8. U.S. Central Intelligence Agency, "World Factbook" (last updated November 17, 2011). www.cia.gov/library/publications/ the-world-factbook/geos/us.html.

9. Madden and Zickuhr, "65% of Online Adults Use Social Networks," Pew Internet & American Life Project, August 2011.

10. Phil Matier and Andy Ross, interview, March 22, 2007.

11. Andrew Ross, interview, September 2, 2011.

12. Matier and Ross, interview, March 22, 2007.

13. Brad Martin, interview, July 2007.

14. "Clinton's Debate Moment," C-SPAN, 1992 presidential debate, YouTube. www.youtube.com/watch?v=ta_SFvgbrlY.

15. CNN Republican presidential debate, October 18, 2011.
16. George Lakoff, interview, June 12, 2007.
17. Bill Press, e-mail, July 19, 2007.
18. David Brock, e-mail, June 7, 2007. The Media Matters Web site is www.mediamatters.org.
19. Ibid.
20. Kerry Kennedy, interview, April 4, 2007.
21. Fred Ross Sr., "Axioms for Organizers," pamphlet prepared by the Service Employees International Union (SEIU), 2003.

Chapter Seven

1. Chris Finnie, e-mail, July 14, 2007.
2. Jim Zogby, e-mail, May 2007.
3. Alec Bash, interview, March 2007.
4. Thom O'Shaughnessy, e-mail, May 31, 2007.
5. Donnie Fowler, interview, March 7, 2007.
6. Donna Brazile, e-mail, June 4, 2007.

After Action Review

1. Willie L. Brown Jr., interview, March 27, 2007.
2. Wade Randlett, interview, August 11, 2011.

Acknowledgments

Thanks to all the people I have met on the campaign trail since those early days in the stroller. Special thanks to the friends and mentors I met growing up in politics, who taught me how to fight, how to win, how to regroup, and how to persevere. You shaped the insights that went into the making of this book, and the campaign advice that I hope will inform a new generation of leaders.

Deep appreciation to the dozens of contributors who took time from your own service to our country to lend the benefit of your thinking by contributing interviews and insights for the book. As progressives, conservatives, and muckrakers, you do not share a common philosophy, but you do share a similar belief in the power of individuals to shape history and the need for more people to become fully engaged in our democracy. I particularly appreciate the wisdom of my grassroots and netroots allies who are thriving in this new era of asymmetrical politics, bringing old school politics and new media together.

Thanks to the excellent candidates who run for office, putting yourselves out there for what you believe and trying to make a difference for the rest of us. The campaign lessons here are built on the work of the team at AFSCME who help prepare people to fight for people who work for a living: they include Jerry

McEntee, Lee Saunders, Larry Scanlon, Linda Canan Stephens, Ricky Feller, Brian Weeks, and Seth Johnson. Thanks to them and to the campaign mavens at the New House PAC and all my boot camp partners whose trainings in public service elevate candidate trainings to an art form.

This book would not have been possible without my networks, especially the dozens of campaign boot camp conveners who have welcomed Isabella and me into your communities, and organized trainings in your homes, union halls, conferences, and classrooms. A salute to my DNC colleagues and cofounders of the DNC Veterans and Military Families Council, my "HUD women" from Washington, D.C., former Capitol Hill colleagues, California grassroots allies, and Rod Snyder and all the Young Democrats of America. Thanks also to my editors at the *Huffington Post* and POLITICO, to Bernard Ashcraft for making the UC Extension connection, to Lizbeth Hasse for providing legal counsel, and to Brad Martin for training and editing advice. Great thanks to Berrett-Koehler publishers for encouraging this second edition, to Neal Maillet and Kirsten Sandberg for their editorial guidance and BookMatters's Dave Peattie and Tanya Grove.

As always, lots of love to my parents and siblings: Nancy and Paul Pelosi; Nancy Corinne, Jeff, Alexander, and Madeleine Prowda; Jacqueline, Michael, Liam, Sean, and Ryan Kenneally; Paul Pelosi, Jr.; Alexandra, Michiel, Paul, and Thomas Vos; Phil, Octavio, and Isabella Kaufman; and to my extended family.

A final thanks to my wonderful husband, Peter, for all you are and all you do.

Index

Absentee-ballot programs,
    206–207
Action alerts, 183
Advisers for kitchen cabinets, 112
American Federation of State
    County and Municipal
    Employees (AFSCME), 3
Appearance for public events,
    162–163
Arab American Institute, 192
Audio releases, 172

Bachmann, Michelle, 57, 59
Bad news, handling, 110–111
Ballots, understanding, 214–215
Bash, Alec, 193
Bay Area Democrats, 140
Big Daddy's Rules of the Road,
    32–33
Billboards, 175
Binah, Rachel, 137, 139–140
Blogs for communication plans,
    172–173
Bloomberg, Michael, 142
Blue Dog Coalition, 89
Blumenthal, Richard, 59

Boggs, Lindy, 38
Boot camp model, 2–3. *See also*
    Campaign boot camps
Boxer, Barbara, 116–117, 139
Braley, Bruce, 88
Brazile, Donna, 126, 127, 212
Broadcast television, 169
Brown, Charlie, 45
Brown, Jan, 45
Brown, Jerry, 65
Brown, Scott, 122
Brown, Willie L., Jr., 105
"Brown Brigade," 122
Bus Project, 92

Cable television, 169–170
Cain, Herman, 58
Call sheets, 148–149
Call to service, 11–12. *See also*
    Public service
    articulating vision for future
        and, 13
    assembling policy act for, 35–40
    and building networks, 20–21
    personal, 11–12
    skeletons and, 40

Call to service *(continued)*
  strengthening friendships and
    networks for, 18–20
  What You Say about You and,
    51–53
Campaign boot camps, 2–3
  convening, 205
  Get Real exercise for, 216–217
Campaign calendar, example of,
  194
Campaign counsel, job description
  for, 106
Campaign kickoff events, 168
Campaign manager, 101–102
  budgets and, 123
  job description for, 106
Campaign pledges and questionnaires, 57
Campaign skills, 124–125
Campaign staff
  job descriptions for, 106–107
  managing, 103–111
  nimbleness and, 105, 108
  recruiting, 109–110
  strategic thinking and, 105
Campaign staff and volunteer
  leadership teams, 103–104
Campaigning, negative, 57–58
Campaigns, 2, 96
  e-mails for announcing, 193
  home stretch of, 211
  issues bonds for, 61–62
  surprises/setbacks and, 110–111
  throwing and taking punches
    in, 191
  values bonds for, 61–62
  winning, 2
Campus networks, 91
Canvassing operations
  checklist for launching, 199–200
  setting up, 198
  for voter contact, 203

Chandler, Ben, 196
Chávez, César, 116
Christensen, Clayton M., 36–37
*Citizens United v. Federal Election
  Commission*, 60–61
Cleland, Max, 70–71, 152, 154
Clemens, Alex, 96–97
Clinton, Bill, 108, 211
Clinton, Hillary Rodham, 116
Coalition networks, 90
Coalitions, including primary foes
  in, 93
Colbert, Stephen, 54–55
Cold prospecting, 150
College Democrats, 91
College Republicans, 91
Collegiate Network, 91
Communication plans. *See* Mes-
  sage communications plans
Communications director, job
  description for, 107
Communities, 79
  geography of, 80–81
  having visceral understanding of,
    96, 100
  identifying networks in, 90–93
  identifying opinion leaders in,
    82
  identifying traditions of, 80–81
  targeting supporters in, 94–96
  understanding people living in,
    80
Community Inventory, 117, 138,
  144
  preparing a, 79–85, 97–100
Community outreach, 114
Community service leaders
  connecting with, 100
  Get Real exercise, 100
  networking with, 85–89
Community weeklies, 174
Constitution, Preamble to, 11

Corporate personhood. *See Citizens United v. Federal Election Commission*

Crider, Jennifer, 142–143

Criticism and effectiveness, 39–40

Crowd-source ideas, 147

Cuomo, Andrew, 73

Daily Kos, 84–85

D'Alesandro, Nancy, 92

D'Alesandro, Thomas, Jr., 70

Database manager, job description for, 107

Debates, preparing for, 182–183

DemocracyAction network, 193

Dialing for dollars, 148–149. *See also* Phone banks

Direct mail, 175

for fund-raising, 150–151

Don't Ask, Don't Tell (DADT) policy, 15–17

Drinan, Robert F., 38–39

Drivers for Election Day operations, 213–214

Durst, Will, 165, 184

Dyer, Jeff, 37

E-mail(s)

for announcing campaigns, 193

as fund-raising tools, 151–154

netiquette for, 74

Economy, knowing the, 80

Edwards, John, 116

Elderly. *See* Seniors networks

Election Day operations, 212

documenting, 215

drivers for, 213–214

field directors and, 212

passers and, 213

phoners for, 214

pollwatchers and, 213

precinct captains and, 212–213

protecting your vote and, 214–215

solving problems and, 215

teams for, 212

Election protection teams, 104, 212–214

Get Real exercise for enlisting, 130

mobilizing, 125–128

Emerge America, 166

EMILY's List, 27

Eshoo, Anna, 119

Ethics

following your personal code of conduct, 28–29

research and, 56

Etiquette. *See also* Netiquette

at public events, 163

Events for fund-raising, 149–150

Facebook, 44, 173

Family, 42–43, 112

Federal Election Commission (FEC), 144

Feinstein, Dianne, 65

Field director

Election Day operations and, 212

job description for, 106

Field offices, opening, 201–202

Field operations

goals for, 201

hiring organizers for, 201

objectives of, 201

planning, 201–202

tools for, 202

Field organizers, hiring, 201

Fighting Dems (military veterans), 71

Finance chairs, 120

Finance council, 104, 120–123

Get Real exercise for developing, 129–130

recruiting members of, 121

Finance director, 120
  job description for, 107
Finance reports, filing, 154–156
Finnie, Chris, 189
Foley, Mark, 75
Follow-up
  importance of, 205
  letters, 185–186
Fowler, Donnie, 95–96, 196
Friend-raising, 87
Friends, first-name *vs.* last-name,
  111
Friendships, strengthening
  for call to service, 18–20
Fund-raising, 135–137. *See also*
  Fund-raising tools
  asking for money, 139–140
  borrowing money and, 144
  elements of plans for, 141–146
  establishing control mechanisms
    for, 142–143
  filing finance reports and,
    154–156
  forecasting needs and, 141–142
  Get Real exercise for, 156–158
  identifying prospective donors
    for, 144
  identifying tools for, 145
  kits for, 146
  matching donors with tools and
    target dollars, 145–146, 158
  online, 151–154
  understanding why people give,
    135–138
Fund-raising opportunities, offering a variety of, 140
Fund-raising tools. *See also*
  Fund-raising
  dialing for dollars, 148–149
  direct mail solicitation for,
    150–151
  e-mails as, 151–154
  meetings and events, 149–150
  phone banks, 150
  varying, 148–154

Geography
  of communities, understanding,
    80–81
  Get Real exercise for mapping
    political, 97–100
Gergersen, Hal, 37
Get-out-the-vote rallies, 207, 211
Get-out-the-vote strategies
  absentee-ballot programs,
    206–207
  early voting, 206
  schedule for, 208–210
  vote-by-mail programs, 206–207
Get Real exercises
  for building kitchen cabinets,
    129
  for campaign boot camps,
    216–217
  for developing finance councils,
    129–130
  for enlisting election protection
    teams, 130
  mapping political geography,
    97–100
  for message box, 75–76
  for message communications
    plans, 186–188
  public service fitness test, 46–47
  for recruiting house meeting
    hosts, 129
Giffords, Gabrielle, 34, 178
Gillibrand, Kirsten, 52
Gladwell, Malcolm, 82
Gonzalez, Jim, 105
Google searching your name, 51
Gore, Al, 211
Guadalupe Organization (GO),
  164

Hackett, Paul, 152
Harris, Kamala D., 31, 34
Help, asking strangers for, 30–31
Henderson, Wade, 128
Heritage Foundation, 91
High-intensity voter contact,
    203–204
    canvassing for, 203
    open feedback loop for, 205
    phoning for, 204
Honda, Mike, 190
Horse race numbers, 66
House calls, best practices for,
    196–198
House meeting hosts, 104, 113,
    116–117, 120
    Get Real exercise for, 129
House meetings, components of
    successful, 114–115
Hughes, Mary, 35, 53, 80–81
Human networks, 20, 90
Hurricane Katrina, 5

Ideas
    communicating, for realizing
        your vision, 13–14
    testing, 15–17
Incumbents, running against, 83
Innovative thinking, 36–37
Intercollegiate Studies Institute
    (ISI), 91
Internet. See also specific topics
    searching one's name on the, 51
Internet research, 60
Iraq war of 2003, 5
Issues bonds, for campaigns, 61–62

Job descriptions for campaign staff,
    106–107
Johnson, Hank, 118

Kantor, Mickey, 110

Katz, Leslie, 124
Kennedy, Kerry, 29
Kickoff events, campaign, 168
King, Martin Luther, III, 116
Kitchen cabinet, 104, 111, 117
    advisers for, 112
    considerations for building,
        111–112
    Get Real exercise for, 129
Kleinfeld, Rachel, 71
Knocking on doors, 23
    best practices for, 196–198
Kumar, Maria Teresa, 127
Kyl, Jon, 54–55

Lakoff, George, 64
Language, use of
    in messages, 62–66
LaRocco, Larry, 118
Latinos, 126–127
Leadership Institute, 91
Leadership qualities, 104–105,
    108–111
    defining oneself vs. being
        defined, 48–49
Leadership role, choosing a
    consider what others say about
        you, 40–41
    consider what others will say
        about you, 43–45
    consult your family, 42–43
Leadership teams
    campaign staff and volunteer
        teams, 103–111
    confident leaders pick competent,
        102–103
    election protection teams, 104,
        125–128
    finance council, 104, 120–123
    Get Real exercise for, 128–131
    house meeting hosts, 104, 113,
        116–117, 120

Leadership teams *(continued)*
  kitchen cabinets, 104, 111–112
  volunteer corps, 104, 123–125
Lee, Barbara, 118
Legal counsel, job description for,
  106
LeMieux, Dotty, 60, 70, 90, 101
Letters to editors, 184
Listening, 167
"Lit drops," 203
Literature
  for field operations, 202
  leafleting, 203
  "lit drops" for, 203
Live airtime, for communication
  plans, 172
Low-intensity activities, for voter
  contact, 203–205
Low-intensity voter contact, 203
Luntz, Frank, 64

Macaca moment, 166
Maffei, Dan, 97
Malcolm, Ellen, 27
Mark, David, 57, 58
Martin, Brad, 62, 93
McEntee, Gerald W., 85–87
McMahon, Linda, 59
McNerny, Jerry, 52
McNerny, Michael, 52
Media
  engaging supporters to interact
    with, 183–185
  monitoring bias in, 184–185
  strengths of, 169
  working with, 177–182
Media Matters of America, 185
Media plan, developing a, 168–177
  arc of the narrative, 168
Meir, Golda, 112
Mentoring, 23–24, 112
Message box, 198

exercises for, 50–51, 75–76
integrating research and polling
  into, 69–70
Message communications plans, 168
  audio releases for, 172
  balancing media mix for,
    176–177
  billboards for, 175
  blogs for, 172–173
  broadcast television for, 169
  cable television for, 169–170
  community weeklies for, 174
  direct mail for, 175
  Get Real exercise for, 186–188
  live airtime and, 172
  newspapers for, 173–174
  phone banks for, 176
  radio ads for, 171–172
  radio for, 171
  texting for, 176
Messages. *See also* Message box
  aggressive scheduling for
    advancing, 71–73
  cultivating experts and allies to
    help deliver, 53–56
  defining, 49
  delivery, 163
  refining, 49–50, 66–68
  research for developing, 59–60
  schedulers and, 72–73
  throwing/taking punches and,
    70–71
  use of language and, 62–66
  walking your talk and, 29–30
Microtargeting, 95
Miller, George, 118–119
Mobile devices, videos that play
  on, 170
Money, asking for, 139–140. *See
  also* Fund-raising
  elements of, 147
Moulitsas, Markos, 84, 87

Murphy, Chris, 149–150, 154

Nana Brigade, 95
Netiquette, 74–75
    for online fund-raising, 151–154
Networking, 24–25
    with community service leaders,
        85–89
Networks
    for call to service, 18–21
    campus, 91
    coalition, 90
    human, 20, 90
    technology, 18–20
    for volunteer corps, activating,
        189–191
    youth, 92
Newmark, Craig, 122
Newsom, Gavin, 31, 34
Newspapers, for message commu-
    nications plans, 173–174
9/11 terrorist attacks, 13
NORAD (North American
    Aerospace Defense Command)
    test, 16

Obama, Barack, 13, 90, 116, 140, 179
Office of Personnel Management
    (OPM), 103
One, Rule of, 44
Online communities, virtual tours
    of. See Networking
Online fund-raising, 151–154
Online operations director, job
    description for, 107
Open feedback loop, 198
    for good/bad news, 167–168
    for voter feedback, 205
Opinion leaders, identifying in
    communities, 82
Opponents, rematches and. See
    Incumbents, running against

O'Shaughnessy, Thom, 195

Paradigms, changings, 68–69
Passers, for Election Day opera-
    tions, 213
Pawlenty, Tim, 59
Pelosi, Nancy, 17, 19, 33, 37, 54, 118
Perlmutter, Ed, 23
Perriello, Mark, 128
Phone banks, 176
    for fund-raising, 150
    for voter contact, 204
Phoners, for Election Day opera-
    tions, 214
Planned Parenthood, 54–55, 68–69
Policy
    balancing purist vs. pragmatic, 37
    knowing the consequences of, 36
    mastering, 36
    teamwork and, 24–25
Policy challenges, mastering the,
    36
Policy director, job description for,
    107
Polis, Jared, 43
Political campaigns. See
    Campaigns
Political geography, Get Real
    exercise for mapping, 97–100
Political risks, taking, 31, 34
POLITICO, 58, 178
Politics, 1
    in communities, understanding,
        83–84
    shoe leather, 196–200
    teamwork and, 24–25
Poll watchers, Election Day opera-
    tions and, 213
Polling
    integrating, into message box,
        69–70
    for refining messages, 66–68

Polls, 66–68
    benefits of good, 66
    early, 66
    media coverage of, 66
    tracking, 66
Pope, Carl, 61–63
Posters, personalized, 119
Pragmatists, policy and, 37
Preamble to U.S. Constitution, 11
Precinct captains, 198–200
    Election Day operations and,
        212–213
Press conferences, checklist for, 181
Primary foes, including in coali-
    tions, 93
Public events
    dressing for, 162
    etiquette and, 163
Public Interest Research Group, 91
Public service. *See* Call to service
Public Service Fitness Test, 46–47
Public speaking, 165–166
    advance work for, 165
    staying on message and, 165–166
Punches, throwing and taking,
    70–71
Purists, policy and, 37

Radio, 171
    live airtime, 172
    talk shows, calling to, 184
Radio ads, 171–172
Rallies, get-out-the-vote, 207, 211
Randlett, Wade, 140
Reagan, Ronald, 93
Republicans, Tea Party, 5, 6
Research
    checklist for opposition, 61
    documenting, 59–60
    ethics and, 56
    integrating into message box,
        69–70

    on Internet, 60
    updating, 59–60
Research director, job description
    for, 107
Research tactics, dirty, 59
Résumés, 40, 59
Richards, Ann, 135
Risk taking, political, 31, 34
RocktheVote.org, 91
Rodriguez, Arturo, 116
Roemer, Tim, 38
Romney, Mitt, 60
Roosevelt, Eleanor, 31
Ross, Fred, Jr., 113
Rule of One, 44

Sacred cows, challenging, 34–35
SaveDarfur.org, 91
Scaife, Richard Mellon, 55
Scanlon, Larry, 104, 105
Scheduler, job description for, 106
Schedulers as message managers,
    72–73
Scheduling for advancing mes-
    sages, 71–73
Schultz, Debbie, 88–89
Seniors networks, connecting with,
    92–93
September 11, 2001 attacks, 13
Service, building a culture of, 20.
    See also Call to service
Service Employees International
    Union (SEIU), 164
SFUsualSuspects.com, 96
Shoe leather politics, 196–200
Showing up
    appearance and, 162
    etiquette and, 163
Sierra Club, 62
Signs, for field operations, 202
Simmons, Jamal, 52, 110
SoCall Grassroots network, 195

Social networks, knowing the, 84–85

Social Security, 93

Strategic thinking
  campaign staffs and, 105
  elements of, 105

Strider, Burns, 32–33

Success, keys to, 219–220

Supporters, targeting, 94–96

Swift Boat Veterans for Truth, 70

Tagaris, Tim, 87

Talk radio shows, calling to, 184

Talkers.com, 171

Talking to people
  Big Daddy's Rules of the Road
    for, 32–33
  knocking on doors, 23

Tea Party, 5, 6

Teamwork
  policy and, 24–25
  politics and, 24–25

Technology networks, 18–20

Television
  broadcast, 169
  cable, 169–170

Texting, 176

Thank-you letters, 185–186
  fundraising and, 149
  for volunteers, 195

"Think Outside Your Bubble" ad, 69

Thompson, Mike, 89

Tierney, John, 89

Torres, Art, 103

Tracking polls, 66

Traditions, identifying in communities, 80–81

Training, 22–23

Treasurer, 120
  job description for, 107

Truman National Security Project,
  71

Trust, 89

United Farm Workers (UFW), 116

Usual Suspects Web site, 96

Valenti, Jack, 36

Values
  following your personal code of
    conduct, 28–29
  testing, 15–17
  vision for future and, 14

Values bonds, for campaigns, 61–62

Veterans for Kerry, 174

Videos, 119, 170

Visibility activities, for voter
  contact, 203

Vision for future
  acts of courage for achieving,
    30–31, 34–35
  articulating, 13
  communication ideas for real-
    izing, 13–14
  testing, 15–17
  values and, 14
  ways of achieving, 17–18

Volunteer coordinator, job description for, 107

Volunteer corps, 104, 123–125
  activating networks for, 189–191
  keeping, 191–196
  recruiting, 189–191
  tracking, 196

Volunteer corps coordinators,
  123–125

Volunteering, 12, 17–18

Vote-by-mail programs, 206–207

Voter contact
  creative examples of, 203
  high-intensity, 203–204
  low-intensity, 203
  mixing low- and high-intensity
    activities for, 203–205

Voter files, 94–96
Voter-identification programs,
    204–205
Voting
    early, 206
    registering to vote, 21–22
Voting rights, 126, 214
Voting systems, understanding,
    215

Walking your talk, messages and,
    29–30
Walz, Tim, 190
Wellstone, Paul, 50, 69
Westine, Lezlee, 17–18, 20, 110,
    123

Whitman, Meg, 120
Will, George F., 13, 104
Winning, keys to, 219–220
Wolff, Brian, 147, 148
Women candidates
    tips for, 26
    voter attitudes toward, 28
Women leaders, 24–28
    taking on sacred cows, 34–35
Wyman, Rosalind "Roz," 24, 119

Yearly Kos, 84–85
Young America's Foundation, 91
Youth networks, 92

Zogby, James, 191, 192

About the Author

Drew Altizer Photography

Attorney, author, and activist Christine Pelosi has a lifetime of grassroots organizing and public policy experience. She conducts leadership boot camps based on her book *Campaign Boot Camp: Basic Training for Future Leaders* (2007), which emerged from her years of grassroots activism and service with the AFSCME PEOPLE/New House PAC Congressional Candidates Boot Camp, which worked with approximately 100 challengers from 2006 to 2010, 26 of whom were elected to Congress.

Her second book, *Campaign Boot Camp 2.0* (2012), draws from her trainings with candidates, volunteers, and NGO leaders in over thirty states and three countries, her classroom experience teaching Public Service Leadership Boot Camp for UC Extension in San Francisco, and her frequent blogging at the *Huffington Post* and POLITICO's *Arena*. It details the role of social media, the Web, and technology in politics and explores the unique leadership challenges for women candidates.

Christine holds a JD from the University of California Hastings College of the Law and a BSFS from Georgetown University's School of Foreign Service. She has served as executive director of the CA Democratic Party, deputy city attorney and assistant district attorney for the City of San Francisco, HUD special counsel in the Clinton-Gore administration, and chief of staff to U.S. Congressman John F. Tierney. Christine chairs the California Democratic Party Women's Caucus, led the California Democratic Party Platform Committee for thirteen years, has been elected four times to the Democratic National Committee, where she cofounded the DNC Veterans and Military Families Council and serves as a vice chair, and serves on the Stakeholder Board of the Young Democrats of America.

An avid baseball fan, she lives within walking distance of her beloved World Champion San Francisco Giants and serves on the Giants Community Fund board of directors. She is married to filmmaker Peter Kaufman; their daughter Isabella was born in 2009.

Berrett–Koehler
BK Publishers

Berrett-Koehler is an independent publisher dedicated to an ambitious mission: *Creating a World That Works for All*.

We believe that to truly create a better world, action is needed at all levels—individual, organizational, and societal. At the individual level, our publications help people align their lives with their values and with their aspirations for a better world. At the organizational level, our publications promote progressive leadership and management practices, socially responsible approaches to business, and humane and effective organizations. At the societal level, our publications advance social and economic justice, shared prosperity, sustainability, and new solutions to national and global issues.

A major theme of our publications is "Opening Up New Space." Berrett-Koehler titles challenge conventional thinking, introduce new ideas, and foster positive change. Their common quest is changing the underlying beliefs, mindsets, institutions, and structures that keep generating the same cycles of problems, no matter who our leaders are or what improvement programs we adopt.

We strive to practice what we preach—to operate our publishing company in line with the ideas in our books. At the core of our approach is stewardship, which we define as a deep sense of responsibility to administer the company for the benefit of all of our "stakeholder" groups: authors, customers, employees, investors, service providers, and the communities and environment around us.

We are grateful to the thousands of readers, authors, and other friends of the company who consider themselves to be part of the "BK Community." We hope that you, too, will join us in our mission.

A BK Currents Book

This book is part of our BK Currents series. BK Currents books advance social and economic justice by exploring the critical intersections between business and society. Offering a unique combination of thoughtful analysis and progressive alternatives, BK Currents books promote positive change at the national and global levels. To find out more, visit **www.bkconnection.com**.

Berrett–Koehler
BK Publishers

A community dedicated to creating
a world that works for all

Visit Our Website: www.bkconnection.com

Read book excerpts, see author videos and Internet movies, read
our authors' blogs, join discussion groups, download book apps, find
out about the BK Affiliate Network, browse subject-area libraries of
books, get special discounts, and more!

Subscribe to Our Free E-Newsletter, the *BK Communiqué*

Be the first to hear about new publications, special discount offers,
exclusive articles, news about bestsellers, and more! Get on the list
for our free e-newsletter by going to **www.bkconnection.com**.

Get Quantity Discounts

Berrett-Koehler books are available at quantity discounts for orders
of ten or more copies. Please call us toll-free at (800) 929-2929 or
email us at bkp.orders@aidcvt.com.

Join the BK Community

BKcommunity.com is a virtual meeting place where people from
around the world can engage with kindred spirits to create a world
that works for all. BKcommunity.com members may create their own
profiles, blog, start and participate in forums and discussion groups,
post photos and videos, answer surveys, announce and register for
upcoming events, and chat with others online in real time. Please join
the conversation!

Certified

Corporation
bcorporation.net